Jesus Lost

and Found

Resurrected for Real 2,000 Years Later!

By Eileen McCourt

Jesus Lost and Found

Resurrected for Real 2,000 Years Later!

By Eileen McCourt

CONTENTS

ABOUT THE AUTHOR

Eileen McCourt is a retired school teacher of English and History with a Master's degree in History from University College Dublin.

She is also a Reiki Grand Master teacher and practitioner, having qualified in Ireland, England and Spain, and has introduced many of the newer modalities of Reiki healing energy into Ireland for the first time, from Spain and England.

Eileen holds regular workshops and healing sessions in Elysium Wellness, Newry, County Down; New Moon Holistics N.I. Carrickfergus, County Antrim; Angel Times, Limerick.

This is Eileen's tenth book.

Previous publications include:

- *'Living the Magic'*, published in December 2014

- *'This Great Awakening'*, September 2015

- *'Spirit Calling! Are You Listening?'*, January 2016

- *'Working With Spirit: A World of Healing'*, January 2016

- *'Life's But A Game! Go With The Flow!'*, March 2016

- *'Rainbows, Angels and Unicorns!'*, April 2016

- *'........And That's The Gospel Truth!'*, September 2016

- *'The Almost Immaculate Deception! The Greatest Scam in History?'*, September 2016

- *'Are Ye Not Gods?' The true inner meanings of Jesus' teachings and messages'*, March 2017

Eileen has also recorded 6 guided meditation cds with her brother, pianist Pat McCourt:

- *'Celestial Healing'*

- *'Celestial Presence'*

- *'Cleansing, energising and balancing the Chakras'*

- *'Ethereal Spirit'*

- *'Open the Door to Archangel Michael'*

- *'Healing with Archangel Raphael'*

All publications are available from Amazon online and all publications and cds are in Angel and Holistic centres around the country, as specified on the website.

Website: www.celestialhealing8.co.uk

ACKNOWLEDGEMENTS

I wish to thank, yet again, my publishers, Don Hale OBE and Dr. Steve Green for their advice and input.

And my sincere thanks, yet again, to my family and my wonderful friends for their constant support and encouragement.

Sincere and heart-felt appreciation to all of you who are buying my books and cds and for your kind comments. I am just happy that my books are helping you on your Spiritual path!

Thank you to all who attend my workshops and courses, and to all who have taken the time to write reviews for me, both in my books and on Amazon. You are greatly appreciated!

To Ozark Mountain Publishing, thank you for permission to quote specific material "Jesus and the Essenes" by Dolores Cannon published by Ozark Mountain Publishing, LLC, Huntsville, AR. 2001

And as always, I give thanks for all the great blessings that are constantly being sent our way in this wonderful, loving, abundant Universe.

Peace be with you!

Eileen McCourt

7th July 2017

NOTE TO READER

Please note, that in keeping with modern scholarly designations in dating, I have used throughout this book C.E. instead of A.D. and B.C.E. instead of B.C.

C.E. means **Common Era** and refers to the years from the beginning of the first century onwards to modern times.

B.C.E. means **Before the Common Era** and refers to the years before the first century.

Also, for the sake of clarity, I have referred to the canonical gospels just simply as Matthew, Mark, Luke and John, even though those gospels were not written by those particular named persons. These are just the names by which we know and recognise them.

And speaking of names! **Jesus** is the name presented to us in the gospels and in all church teachings, and it is by that name that we recognise him. However, that is the Romanised version of Jesus' real name, confirmed by the Council of Nicaea in 325 C.E., all other names being declared heresy. Jesus' real name, the name by which he was known when he lived on earth 2,000 years ago, was **Yeshua,** Yeshua ben Joseph, Yeshua son of Joseph. I have used both names throughout this book, and in no particular pattern, just to remind the reader that Yeshua was the real name. At the same time, however, it matters not in the Spirit world what name anyone goes by. A name is only a label, an identification marker, for this earth dimension only. In Spirit, names are irrelevant. There, it is all thought processing. Yeshua, known to us as Jesus, is now known to us as **Sananda** in the higher planes.

Josephus, the first-century Jewish historian, whose work is prevalent throughout this book, refers to Jesus only twice in all of his works, and one of those is now widely regarded by scholars as an interpolation, known as the '*Testimonium Flavianum*', and which has led many people to believe that Jesus never existed. However, Josephus did write about Jesus, under the name **Wonderworker.**

The **Essene Brotherhood,** the secretive and mysterious sect of Judaism, of whom Jesus was a member, are not mentioned in the canonical gospels under that name. You will find them referred to as **Nazoreans**, a branch of the Essenes, just like the **Ebionites,** or the **Therapeutae,** this latter mostly near Alexandria in Egypt. Hence, contrary to widespread belief, **Jesus the Nazorean** does not mean **Jesus from Nazareth,** but **Jesus the Essene.**

Capital letters have been used throughout to symbolise the specific, as distinct from the generic. For example, spiritual, church, bishop, pope, gospels, gods, doctrines, in general do not warrant a capital letter, but when spoken of in the specific, as for example, the Christian Church, the Gospel of Philip, the Crucifixion of Jesus, the Spirit world, the Spiritual path, then a capital letter is warranted.

Likewise, when referring to the worldwide institution known as the Christian Church or the Roman Catholic Church, I have used capitals throughout, but when referring to the church in general, then I have refrained from such usage.

Eileen McCourt

7th July 2017

REVIEWS

I must confess to being something of a 'fan' of the writings of Eileen McCourt. I find her approach and dedication to her topics fervent and refreshing. She has a 'no fear' attitude to her work. Neither however, is she cavalier in her approach. In fact, she is most certainly responsible and clinical in her research and unflinching in her coverage of all the material. 'Jesus Lost and Found' is no exception, in which McCourt uncovers a 'Da Vinci Code' like trail of deception to undermine the real teachings and beauty of Jesus' message.

McCourt argues that Jesus has become lost in the opulence and splendour of the Vatican, in the Michelangelo and the Bernini, in the Church that carries his name. More so, McCourt suggests that Jesus wasn't so much lost, but hidden, obscured for social and political gain. As history is written by the victors, so, it would appear, is Jesus' story. Re-written by the dominant religious organisation, as a manifestation of their political and philosophical ideology. Viewed through the lens of their structures of dominance and control.

McCourt suggests, however, that we take a step back and view a Jesus that is separate from this multi-national conglomerate of 'Christianity' and look to the uncomplicated prophet of Galilee and his simple message of love and oneness. If this indeed is the age of spiritual revealing, as the ancients would have us believe, this must be an aspect of it. Unfortunately, in the modern age, Jesus' name has become synonymous with control and hypocrisy through the dogmas and demands of the Church. McCourt is intent on wrestling this false image cleanly out of the hands of the manipulative.

Jesus, or Yeshua Ben Joseph, was clearly not a 'rules man', as the

Church would have us believe. Rather, he was a figure for change and hope, evolving from the revolutionary Essenes community, how could he be any other? McCourt contends that Yeshua's message remains revolutionary and relevant to this very day, never the staid and stifling ideology of fear and punishment. Jesus' message is of the beauty and interconnectedness of the soul and the all encompassing love of the Great Spirit.

'Jesus Lost and Found' is a riveting read, challenging in parts, but thoroughly life and soul-enhancing in totality. Jesus' message is essential to us, more so now than ever. It would be a great loss to the soul, if we allowed Yeshua's message to be usurped and undermined. McCourt has indeed found Jesus amid the Machiavellian machinations of the corrupt and greedy. 'Jesus Lost and Found' is a 'ray of hope'. A timely message and an inspiring vision!

Declan Quigley, Shamanic Practitioner and co-founder of The Irish School of Shamanic Studies

A most inspiring book about the life and teachings of the real man behind Jesus. Proposing that Jesus, aka Yeshua ben Joseph, was but one member of the secretive Essene society and had access to a wealth of hidden spiritual knowledge, the author suggests that Jesus used this knowledge to divinely educate the people through narrative parables.

She further advocates that this divine education in conjunction with writings from the Old Testament allowed Jesus the man to fulfil the prophecies and to be crucified on the cross, all in the name of Truth.

The caveat however, is that the author does not believe that Jesus actually died on the cross but was removed by gathering Essenes and treated back to good health. The author's arguments are very sound and should be treated with the utmost respect and gravity.

This is a serious book that will magically inform yet allow the reader to decipher and digest the factual life and times of the real man behind the mask of the Christian Jesus.

Worth every penny and more!

Clare Bowman (Spiritual Historian)

It is indeed the truth that will set us free, and McCourt has once again produced a convincing argument that relies on historical research and logic, and not the unfettered interpretation of what has come to be known as 'alternative facts'.

All actions can only be assessed reliably through interpretation within cultural context, and this is where the McCourt ship sails majestic. As with previous attempts to enlighten the murky waters of politico/religious contemporaneous reporting, McCourt has again wielded the scalpel of fact-based analysis with the precision and clarity of a surgeon, which has resulted in a riveting read, cover to cover.

McCourt provides significant food for thought for those who are willing to open their eyes in the ongoing evasive pursuit of truth in an era of post truth!!

P.M. (Psychologist)

Another wonderful book by you, Eileen!

You open your eyes to the truth!

Thank you, and thanks for the beautiful gift God has given you. It's an honour to call you my friend!

Francesca Brown, Angel Whisperer.

JESUS LOST AND FOUND

FOREWORD

Today, most people have their minds already made up about Jesus. They have a fixed image, and that's it! No shifting!

Faith and historical facts make uneasy bed-fellows! They do not rest easily alongside each other!

The image of the Jesus of faith, the image instilled into us for centuries by orthodox religion, the image of Jesus as a divine being, the only Son of God, endowed with supernatural powers, dying on the cross for our sins and to redeem all mankind, and then being raised from the dead is indeed an image that is difficult to shift. An image of a meek, mild and docile Jesus, exuding unconditional love and forgiveness to friends and enemies alike!

But! In reality, an image far removed from the real Yeshua who walked through the Galilee region 2,000 years ago!

Hence books like this one are looked on by many with suspicion and distrust. There is a certain unease, a certain worry, and it is an understandable worry, that the Jesus portrayed in every new book will not be the Jesus we have all been taught about. A concern that Jesus will be reduced from the deified Divine Son of God, the Jesus with whom we are comfortable, to a mere mortal just like us! We are outside our comfort zone indeed! We are hesitant to entertain the idea and the image of Jesus as any other than what orthodox religion has depicted him to be. There is a fear that something might just be found in all the research that is now going on that might shatter our comfortable belief system. Something that might require a re-thinking! Something that might force us to re-consider! Something that might just make us question! A reassuring and comforting religion, neatly packaged, which promises us so much, but just cannot deliver, and which just does not do what it says on the tin, is still more attractive to so many of us than a challenging form of Spirituality where each and every one of us takes the responsibility for our own soul evolution, our own Spiritual growth and progress, and the Spiritual evolution of all humanity.

Many are up for the challenge. But even more are not yet ready. Not yet ready to discard the old beliefs and shake off the comfortable, well-attached, well-ingrained, well-moulded shackles of centuries of church teachings and dogmas. If you are holding this book, then you are one of the former! You are ready! Indeed, you may well have already discarded those binding shackles!

Well armed now with newly discovered ancient sources, such as the Dead Sea Scrolls, the gospels and writings found at Nag Hammadi, none of which made it into the canonical gospels, long overlooked writings of the early church, new archaeological evidence, modern day past-life regressions and modern day Spiritual channellings, scholars, theologians and biblical historians are reconstructing the life, times and teachings of the man known to us as Jesus of Nazareth, and what they are finding is a Jesus very different from the Jesus traditionally depicted over the last 2,000 years. What we now are being presented with is very different from what we have been led to believe for all that time.

And what we are now being presented with is forcing us to face what could well be, for many of us, our greatest fear. Our greatest fear that Jesus might just turn out to be a composite figure, a created character, manifested through church dogmas, doctrines and teachings to fulfil a particular agenda and purpose.

So what you are about to read may well shock some of you. I am not given to making eccentric claims or creating farcical or unbelievable stories simply in order to sell books. I am a trained historian and teacher by profession, and also a Spiritual author and teacher. I seek the truth, and in this book, as in all my other previous books, I provide evidence and support for everything I write. And again, as before, I simply ask that you consider, within your own intuitive being, what is written in this book and do not just discard what it contains as not being possible. Your own intuition and inner guidance will lead you, as always, to that degree of truth for which you are ready at this moment in time.

We are living in changed and changing times, as long established church, political and fiscal institutions tumble down around us, to be replaced by the not yet known. The good news is, though, that in the midst of all the turmoil, man's unquenchable thirst for the truth continues. Without doubt, one of the most positive attributes of this present age! And the most worthy advances in science and technology have, and are being made in the pursuit of that elusive, yearned-for truth. But there are those who still resist, still unwilling to face that truth! Still clinging to control. Still desperate to get and retain power! *Our power!*

The poet Robert Browning, in his famous poem '*Paracelsus*' wrote:

'Truth is within ourselves; it takes no rise / From outward things, whate'er you may believe. / There is an inmost centre in us all, / Where truth abides in fulness; and around, / Wall upon wall, the gross flesh hems it in, / This perfect, clear perception - which is truth.'

All truths, before being accepted, must now run the gauntlet of abuse, mockery, criticism, being put through the sieve of accountability and logic before being accepted. And it is only right that they should do so! Failure to do so, as has so often happened in the past, results in loss of knowledge, wrong judgements, bias, leading us all up the wrong path, very often even in a backward direction. Simply because the church teaches, propounds or proclaims some new doctrine is no longer sufficient for its acceptance. Those days are gone! Relegated to the dust-bin of history!

In the Gospel of Thomas, one of those gospels found at Nag Hammadi in 1945, and which did not make its way into the New Testament, we read *"There is nothing hidden that will not be revealed"*.

Leonardo da Vinci attempted to get across to us the importance of truth:

'Blinding ignorance does mislead us. O wretched mortals, open your eyes!'

And:

'The noblest pleasure is the joy of understanding.'

And, in the Gospel of Philip, also one of those gospels found at Nag Hammadi in 1945, and which likewise failed to make its way into the canonical gospels, we read:

'While hidden, truth is like ignorance: / It keeps to itself. / But when it is revealed, it is recognised and glorified, / for it is more powerful than ignorance and error. / It brings freedom. / The Logos said: 'If you know the truth, the truth shall make you free.' / Ignorance is slavery, / knowledge is freedom. / When we recognise the truth, we taste its fruits in ourselves. / When we unite with truth, it shares its fullness with us.' (Gospel of Philip, Plate 132)

And yet again:

'Ignorance is the cause of all evil, and serves death. / Nothing has been or ever will be born from ignorance.' (Gospel of Philip, Plate 131)

No wonder gospels such as these were not included in the canonical gospels! Orthodox Christian churches have spent the last 2,000 years keeping the truth well hidden from the masses, reserving it only for the church hierarchies themselves. And no wonder the vast majority of people on earth at this point in time still dwell in the death consciousness state, the lower, most dense of Spiritual energy levels. It is in keeping the masses in that lower state of consciousness, still in their long slumber, still unawakened to the Spiritual truth, that has served orthodox Christian churches so well for so long.

But the spirit of man cannot be chained or tied down! It is that indominatable human spirit, that Spiritual energy force within each human body, that urges man on to face the most daunting of challenges. It is that indominatable human spirit that arises time and time again when the call of the world goes out in times of dire distress. And it is that indominatable human spirit that continues to break down barriers, that continues to explore all avenues, that refuses to surrender in the search for truth! That Spiritual energy force inherent in each and every one of us, our Divine essence, cannot be broken or controlled by outside forces! And that is what orthodox Christian churches have over-looked and neglected to take into account!

So how do we find the truth about the real Jesus? The truth about Yeshua, Yeshua ben Joseph, Yeshua the Nazarene?

In order to find Jesus, the Yeshua of first century Jewish Palestine, we must go back to that period in history, we must rewind the tape and place ourselves very firmly in that setting, completely removed from our present 21st century thinking, our present understandings, our present ideas and concepts. We must release our binding, suffocating, restricting prejudices, our long-held beliefs. We must open our minds, empty our minds, and try to walk in another man's shoes, try to empathise with those who lived at that time, when a Messiah was imminently expected, a Messiah, a Christ, the anointed one, who, it was believed, would free the Jewish people from the oppression of Roman rule. Try to place ourselves in that hot-bed, that smouldering political and religious furnace that was first-century Judaea and Galilee, a land oppressed by the expanding Roman Empire; a land where insurrection was sporadic and brutally dealt with; a land where dissent was rife, rumbling away above and below the surface, waiting for this one and only Saviour who was to appear amongst them at any moment now. A land where the knowledge of the Old Testament prophecies was widespread and a land that awaited the imminent fulfilling of those same prophecies.

The prophecies! One of the keys to our understanding of what the life of Yeshua was all about! Those same prophecies that foretold a Saviour born of a virgin; a crucified Saviour; a dying and resurrected Saviour!

And the second vital key to our understanding of what the life of Yeshua was all about? That second vital key is to be found in the Ancient Mystery Schools and the ancient Mystery Teachings! The teachings of Yeshua were the teachings of these Ancient Mystery Schools!

And the third and final key? That other vital key, the key that opens that secret door to our understanding of the life of Yeshua? The secretive and mysterious Essene Brotherhood!

The prophecies of the Old Testament, the Ancient Mystery Schools and their Teachings, and the secretive and mysterious Essene Communities are inter-linked and inter-connected in a way which has mostly been overlooked! And it is through these three vital keys that we can find the real Jesus! It is this Yeshua of first century Jewish Palestine whom this book is seeking to find. And yes! We can find him! Through the ancient prophecies and the secretive, mysterious Essene Brotherhood!

Yeshua is right there, underneath all the rubble of false church doctrine, dogmas and teachings, underneath all the lies and cover-ups, the deceit, the conspiracies, the manipulations, the propaganda, the spin, that deified and mythologised him, removing him from his place in first century Jewish Palestine and placing him in the fabricated, rigged-up setting of the early Roman Christian Church, branded, exploited and framed for power, control and mercenary gain. And we must rid ourselves of the false orthodox church teachings that Jesus died on the cross to redeem mankind from sin. Jesus did not die to redeem us! No man can bear the guilt of the sins of all humanity! Each and every one of us must take responsibility for our own soul development, our own soul evolution, our own soul awareness.

Yeshua never claimed to be the *only begotten son of God*'! And we must not see him as God in God's entirety! That is the greatest scam the Roman Christian Church has perpetrated! We are all of divine essence, just like Yeshua! But we are not God in the totality of God. Orthodox religion has taught about the divinity of Jesus, but it has failed to teach about the divinity of man! Failed to teach about our own divinity, about the kingdom of heaven within each and every one of us! Failed to promote Yeshua as he would have wanted to be promoted, - as a Spiritual teacher and guide for us, someone whom we can emulate and follow. Instead, Jesus has been presented to us as being a deity, so far above us that we will never get to where He is.

We need to find the real Jesus! And yes! He is here, in the pages of this book!

NOT a deified Jesus! NOT a mythologised Jesus! NOT the founder of that new church which came to be known as Christianity! And certainly NOT the founder of the Roman Christian Church! That church that was founded to meet the political and economic requirements of the expanding Roman Empire! That church whose history has been stained with propaganda, bloodshed, religious wars, mass murder, genocide, violation of human rights, discrimination against women, gay people, orphans, those born outside wedlock, those who dared to question or oppose its own scientific dogmas, even those scientific teachings which have long since been proven wrong!

And why NOT?

Because this is NOT what Jesus was or is! Jesus did NOT come to found a new church or a new religion! Those days where we swallowed, verbatim, without question, everything the church told us are over! Gone, gone for good! Buried in the mists of time! Returning no more!

And what is history anyway? Henry Ford put it very succinctly, *"History is bunk"*. And who gets to write it? The winners, of course! Who else is there left alive to write it? And what do they write? They have free licence to spin, distort, manipulate, fabricate, lie, cover up, embellish, change and re-edit.

The time has finally come! The time to find and re-claim the historical Yeshua, the Yeshua who attempted to show us a better way to live, the Yeshua who attempted to show us how to raise our Spiritual consciousness from the base energy level to our own Individualised Christ Consciousness level, but whose teachings have been manipulated and distorted, changed and re-edited down through the centuries by those whose lust for power and control have left us with a world where a mere 5% of the population control a massive 95% of the earth's wealth and resources. A world where over half the people live in poverty, and this ironically, in an abundant universe, where there is ample for all. The exploitation of the many by the few!

The Second Coming of Jesus is indeed imminent! But, like everything else, not quite as the orthodox church has taught! Not quite the terrifying, fear-inducing apocalyptic occurrence facing us all, where we will again be judged and either cast down into hell for all eternity or raised up into heaven to share in the wonders prepared for us there.

The Second Coming of Jesus is the finding of the real Jesus underneath all the deceit, all the lies, all the distortions, and a taking back of that real Jesus into our hearts and lives. The real Yeshua that we find when we strip away all the falsifications as we search through the historical evidence, as we find our inner selves, the kingdom of heaven within each and every one of us, and not the Jesus that religion says was there! Not the deified, mythologised Jesus of faith, but the real Yeshua!

Today we must discontinue our long-held trait of seeing Jesus as exclusive or territorial to any one religious belief system and begin to see him as inclusive and belonging to each and every one of us, regardless of race, colour, creed, culture, or ethnic or religious persuasion.

We are all part of a divine plan, a divine force, a divine intelligence, which is in control of all things, and which we cannot understand with our present limited human thinking. That divine plan is to raise the Spiritual consciousness of all humanity, and the life of Yeshua ben Joseph on Planet Earth 2,000 years ago was one spoke in that wheel of ongoing evolution.

We have been presented with only the external, the outer, the surface meaning of Yeshua's teachings. And why? Simply to prevent us finding the real, the inner meanings which lead us to the truth! We have been presented with teachings interpreted by others who set themselves up as being in charge of our Spiritual welfare and development, and charged an extortionate price for doing so! And what a price we paid for handing over our power! But we are reclaiming our power once again!

We are told in the gospels how Jesus was lost for three days at twelve years of age and then found, preaching in the Temple.

Jesus lost and found!

Lost for three days! And his parents thought that was bad! Jesus has since been lost again, but this time for almost 2,000 years! Now that's what one could call a disaster! An absolute tragedy! And the world has so suffered as a consequence! Humanity has remained stuck in the lower Spiritual energy vibration levels for countless centuries simply because the truths which Yeshua came to teach us have been witheld from us!

Jesus was not *exactly lost* though! Lost suggests something inadvertently misplaced or carelessly mislaid. But Jesus was deliberately hidden, deliberately buried, deliberately concealed from us for 2,000 years underneath all the church rubble and rubbish, underneath all the teachings and dogmas! And all for a reason! To quote Leonardo da Vinci again:

'Many have made a trade of delusions and false miracles, deceiving the multitude!'

But to the horror of those who buried him, Jesus has been found again! Alive and well! After all that time!

Found where?

The truth lies in the detail! The truth lies between the lines! The truth lies behind the lines!

What detail? What lines?

It's all there right in front of us, in the New Testament writings, of course! *If we open our eyes!* And in the writings and gospels found at Nag Hammadi and in the Dead Sea Scrolls! Writings and gospels which have been kept hidden from us in case we should learn the truth!

What was it again that Leonardo da Vinci said?

"O wretched mortals, open your eyes!"

This book deals with the **Resurrection of Jesus.** Not the Resurrection as in the gospel stories, **but the resurrection of the real Yeshua from underneath all the rubble and rubbish under which he has been buried for the last 2,000 years!**

Resurrected indeed! But this time for real!

This book begins with the Crucifixion of Jesus, as related in the canonical gospels. There are many questions we need to ask about the crucifixion, though, as with everything else written in these carefully selected gospels, carefully selected by the early church fathers with their own particular agenda in mind.

Only the bravest of souls would have openly confronted and challenged the powerful forces of Rome and their local fawning puppets, - the Sadducees, the High Priests and the priests of the Temple, who formed the Sanhedrin, the Jewish ruling authority. And Yeshua was one such soul. Yeshua tirelessly opposed them, even going against members of his own family, who did not understand that he was teaching a higher law until after it was all over.

The life of Yeshua ben Joseph, known to us as Jesus the Christ is without question, the greatest mystery and story of all time. There has been no other more controversial figure, no other more written about or talked about through history, no other whose teachings have been hijacked and misused to create division, war and persecution, no other whose words have been so widely manipulated in order to attain power and control.

But the same questions still tantalise theologians, lay people and scholars alike!

Who was Jesus? Where did he gain the esoteric knowledge and wisdom he exhibited and taught throughout his mission? What were the secret teachings he shared with his disciples? Where was he during those eighteen missing years?

But, for the purposes of this book, the most important question of all is, **did Jesus really die on the cross?**

It is around the death of Jesus by crucifixion and his subsequent resurrection that the whole of orthodox Christianity is based.

But what if Jesus did not die on that cross? What if he survived? What if it was all a dramatic set-up?

Such a scenario is drama indeed!

And any good drama requires a setting and time, players, plot and script.

So, what was the setting and time for the drama of the life of Jesus? Where and when would this all take place?

Who were the players? Who were those who would reincarnate with him? Who were those who freely volunteered to play certain roles in this unfolding drama?

What was the plot? What was to happen?

What was the script?

One thing for certain was that there would be no dress rehearsal. This one-off performance had to go according to plan. There could be no re-run! No *'take five'!* This was going out live!

So, audience, please take your seats! The performance is about to begin!

Lights! Camera! Action!

INTRODUCTION

DOWN THE VIBRATIONAL CORRIDOR

MY JOURNEY BEGINS

It is time.

Time for me to begin my journey. My journey, yet again, down through the higher energy vibrational frequency levels, down, down, down, to the dense earth plane energy level, down to the world of matter and form.

I am an unlimited cosmic being. I exist beyond time and space. There are no barriers I cannot cross, no demarcations I cannot transcend.

Hence, I am willingly leaving here for yet another life-time on Planet Earth

And where is here?

Here is not a place as you on the earth plane understand a place to be.

Here is that place you refer to as heaven.

Here is an energy vibrational frequency, unlike your dense earth vibrational frequency where you experience life in physical form, in matter.

Here is an energy vibrational frequency, a sublime, ecstatic state of non-physical matter, amongst all the other multitudinous energy vibrational frequencies that swarm all around in the entirety, in the vastness, in the infinity of creation.

Here, we know only love. Love and Light.

Here, we are devoted to helping other souls achieve what we have achieved, merging with Source, merging into the Light.

All humanity, our brothers and sisters, our extended family, are destined eventually to arrive here with us. But it is taking a very long time. Mankind has lost its way. So many are lost in a Spiritual desert, a Spiritual wilderness, a Spiritual vacuum. So many are in Spiritual exile. They are in no-man's land, consumed by worldly passions and desires. They have lost sight of their divine origins, their connection to Source. They are looking for God in all the wrong places. They have a corrupted view of God as a punishing, judgemental external force, an admonishing figure, to whom they offer blood sacrifices and beg for forgiveness for their sins.

The experiment of Atlantis could not last. Man just could not continue to live a life of wholeness in a physical embodiment. He lost connection with his Spiritual essence, he moved away from his connection to Source. Greed took over. Greed and lust for power. But mostly the self, the ego, the attraction of individuality, separation from the whole.

So now I have chosen, once again, to leave this high energy frequency level to return to the earth plane. My vehicle and personal Gatekeeper have been selected.

But I know what you are thinking!

You are thinking that if we are all helping from this side, and our powers are mind-blowing, so much so that we could return earth to a wonderful state of completeness in the blink of a human eye, then why do I need to return to that most dense of energy vibrational frequencies?

The answer?

Because man has been endowed with that most precious of gifts, that most desirable of gifts, that most sacrosanct of gifts, - free will!

We cannot interfere with man's free will from this side. We must join in as human beings, we must become like them, on their own energy frequency level in order to help them. There is no ascension upwards in all these energy frequency levels beyond the level that each soul earns for itself. So I must descend.

I must walk on the earth plane once again, like many advanced souls have done before me. Like Buddha, the awakened one, like Lao Tzu in China, like Gautama Siddharta in India, and like others who are unknown to humanity. The human world was not yet ready for these evolved souls and the message they brought, so that message became greatly misunderstood and greatly distorted.

I need to return, to be amongst them again. I have already had many physical lives, my soul type being that of psychic revelator. I need to reveal to them, to teach them the truths which they have forgotten. To get them back on the right path. To awaken them to the truth of who and what they really are. To help them to re-remember. To help them shift their consciousness, their Spiritual awareness., which at this point in time is the lowest it has ever been.

In previous incarnations I was twice the Emperor of Atlantis over 33,000 earth years ago and 15,000 earth years ago. I also incarnated as Adam and then Enoch. I was Joseph of Egypt, of the Coat of Many Colours 1,600 years ago and then Joshua, the Hebrew military leader 1,300 earth years ago. 800 earth years ago I was Elisha and 600 earth years ago I was Joshua the High Priest, chosen to fulfil that role for the reconstruction of the Jewish Temple after the return of the Jews from captivity in Babylon. I also had a physical life as King David about 1,000 earth years ago.

Now I am reincarnating yet again on the earth plane. This time I will be known as Yeshua. Yeshua ben Joseph, Yeshua son of Joseph.

So my journey is about to begin.

My journey down to the earth plane. Down the vibrational corridor.

Those who are to be my parents, both highly evolved souls, left some time ago. Because I am descending from this high level of energy vibrational frequency, I need the highest of channels, the highest energy vibrational vehicle to form the bridge for me into the physical world of form and matter. Those who will do this for me will be known as Joseph and Mary. Joseph left first, then Mary. They are bringing with them all the wisdom and experience from their previous lives in the temples of Egypt, though they will not, of course, remember all of this, only what is necessary for this life-time.

They, like me, and like every other soul that incarnates on the earth plane are subject to the laws of that dense energy vibrational frequency level. They too, like every soul, will have the veil pulled down over their eyes to the appropriate thickness. The one to be known as John the Baptiser has just recently left. He too has accepted his mission and will know what to do when the time is right. He was formerly incarnated as Moses, the law bringer, the deliverer of the Ten Commandments. Then he went back to the earth plane as Elijah the prophet. Now I am to follow him by teaching love and forgiveness. And of course, the truth! That is my main mission. To teach once again the truths of the Ancient Mystery Schools. Through me, the prophecies will be fulfilled.

Just recently left too, my twin flame, the one who will be known as The Magdalene. She will be my main anchor on the earth plane, my main support. She will maintain the energy supply for our joint mission. She is the Divine Feminine, and will awaken people out of *their old, rigid, patriarchal beliefs, to a new, fresh understanding of the role of the feminine. She will re-balance the imbalance on the dense vibration that is earth. She will restore the balance between the masculine and the feminine. She will sustain the process that I am to start. We have shared many incarnations together, united spiritually in each of them. We will once again find each other when we manifest on the earth plane. Her energy will feel my presence, her energy will draw me to her. She will know when I am approaching, and will come to meet me. She will learn in the great mystery schools of Egypt while I will learn on my vast travels throughout the Mediterranean lands, India and Gaul, and with the Druids, where I will learn everything I need to know for this great task. Then we will meet once again to begin our joint mission. She is an essential part of this plan. She has taken on a difficult role, a woman in a patriarchal society, but her spirit will shine through, her voice will be heard in times to come when it is most needed. We are a team, twin souls, merged energies, Spiritual partners. Our combined energies, working together in perfect harmony will create an energetic force so powerful that it will seem like a great beacon of light throughout the entire universe.*

When I complete this life on Planet Earth, I will return to this, the highest of energy vibrational frequencies, to a state of completedness, a state of wholeness, a state of complete awareness, a state of total Enlightenment, an Ascended One, with the Great White Brotherhood, that most highly evolved and most advanced service order of teachers, operating throughout many levels and many planetary systems.

Some others who have agreed to play a part have also left before me. Those known on the earth plane as the Essenes are already in position, and have been for some time now, about three hundred years of earth time, along the energy lines of the earth, the ley-

lines, preparing for a massive channelling of energy, and preparing to teach me what I need to know for this life-task. They have been building up a massive support grid-network in preparation for my coming. They will teach me all I need to know for this life-mission.

Others will follow in due course. Yet others will join us along the way, as we descend down the vibrational corridor, down through the increasingly heavier vibrations, becoming more and more dense, until we eventually reach the most dense vibration of all, - Planet Earth. When the time is right, we will all find each other to fulfil the plan, to complete our earthly life mission. Together, we will challenge humanity to raise their awareness, to reach out into new and higher frequencies of consciousness, to attain new perspectives of truth, to understand and accept who and what they really are.

The plan has been instigated. They are expecting a saviour, a Messiah. The prophets have prepared the way. Mechanisms have been put in place. And I am to anchor the Light once more upon the earth plane. The Cosmic Light of Love and Energy, opening up people's heart chakras to unconditional love, showing them a new, Spiritual way to live and connect with each other and with God. Once they find that connection, then their Spiritual awareness will increase, and so too will the collective Spiritual consciousness of all humanity. The downward energy spiral must be stopped and reversed to an upward movement.

I will not be born as a great king. Nor indeed, as a great Roman, one who will teach the world! No! That is not the way this plan has been designed. It will be Galilee, it will be amongst poor peasants and fishermen. To be born a great King would negate the plan entirely. That would make people change their ways and beliefs for all the wrong reasons, from external influences. Change must come from within men's hearts, from within, from themselves, from an identity with their own divine nature.

I have chosen a difficult path. Some will listen to me; most will reject me. They will lie about me, they will manipulate and distort my words, they will use me as a brand for power and control. But nothing is set in stone! They have free will! Anything can happen! We shall see! All I can do is try, all I can do is remind them of the great truths, the great mysteries that were taught so long ago, but have now been forgotten. I cannot force them to accept what I teach. If they do not accept it from me, they will learn it all in other life-times.

If you were told that your current beliefs are incorrect or incomplete, would you want to know? Unfortunately, there are many who will prefer to remain in delusional ignorance, not knowing who they are, where they have come from, where they are going. They prefer to remain in their comfortable state where others take all the responsibility and they just tag along. They will laugh at me and scorn me, as the ignorant always do when they do not understand. Others will open their hearts to the truth, looking for a guide who has already been along that same road. I will be that guide, and those who are ready will find me and listen to my words. But I cannot carry anyone. All I can do is hold the ladder as each one ascends to a higher degree of Spiritual awareness, a higher degree of Spiritual consciousness, each in his own time. I will be there to steady the ladder, and to help back onto the ladder again those who stumble or fall off.

The vibrational corridor is opening up in front of me. I say my good-byes for now. I know this is only a temporary separation. I will return and join my Spiritual family again, my Monad, in a wonderful ecstatic merging of our energies. They will be supporting me all the way on my earthly journey, encouraging me and helping me from the side-lines, from this side of the veil.

I start my descent. I have quite a long way to go before I begin to decrease my awareness, my consciousness. There are a lot of levels here in the Spirit world! It is a long descent from my present level of Spiritual consciousness, where we know only Love and Light, down to the most dense of all, the earth plane.

I am aware of other energies joining me, coming along with me. All kind, brave and generous souls who have agreed to play some part or other in this great plan to help humanity. Amongst them are those who will betray me, reject me, crucify me. But they will not know what they do. They will not know, in their earth consciousness, what they do. That is the way it is. That is the way it all works. That is the way it is all designed to work. The prophecies must be fulfilled. The truth must be taught.

I feel myself becoming less light, getting heavier and heavier as I descend down through the different energy dimensions. I am slowing down.......my consciousness is changing............my awareness is dulling............

WHOOSH!

I am in the confined space of my mother's womb. The bridge that joins the Spirit world to the world of matter. The divine feminine! The mother energy! The channel between worlds, the joining link between the worlds of Light and the dense world of matter and form. The gateway for the Spiritual beings of light to enter the dense earth plane energy level.

I still feel very strongly my connection to those worlds of Light that I have just left. My disconnection will be a gradual thing. But it will not be a total disconnection. I will slowly come to find my place in my new life. And when my baby body sleeps, I can escape back again into my totality.

And so a child is born.

The date? Early April in the year 4 B.C.E.

The place? Aramaic-speaking Jewish Palestine.

Jewish Palestine, controlled by Imperial Rome.

Jewish Palestine, ruled by Herod, the Roman client King, who saw himself as King of the Jews.

The child who would be known as Yeshua, - later Romanised to Jesus, becoming the most famous man in history. The man whose name and story would be exploited, distorted and manipulated by those hungry for power and control, turning him into a God, founding the so-called Christian church in his name. That same church that would bring torture, suffering and death in the most horrific forms to millions of people, all in the name of God and of Jesus. That same church that would tolerate no opposition, no other creed or beliefs except their own, castigating all others as heretics, all to be annihilated.

But all that was for the future.

Let us now follow Yeshua's story.

A story of love and compassion.

A story of political intrigue, rejection, hatred, suspicion, deceit and betrayal.

A story of suffering and crucifixion.

A story of gross distortion and manipulation.

A story of.............

Well, let us see!

PART ONE: THE END?

CHAPTER 1

WHY WAS JESUS CRUCIFIED?

Many a good novel or drama starts with the ending. Surely that spoils it for us, one could claim! Conversely, starting with the ending can also enhance it for us. Knowing how it all ends leaves us perplexed, intrigued and wondering how and why it ends in that particular way.

Such texts include Shakespeare's '*Romeo and Juliet*' where we know from the very beginning that the two '*star-cross'd lovers*' are going to die at the end; Willie Russell's '*Blood Brothers*' where we again know the twins are going to die and Jennifer Johnston's novel '*How Many Miles to Babylon?*' which begins with Lieutenant Alexander Moore awaiting his death by execution during World War One. Knowing right from the very beginning how all of these end is a clever technique to get us interested, and exercise our brains to figure out how and why it all happened in that way.

So I now begin this book with the Crucifixion of Jesus, that part of his life which the gospels proclaim as the ending of his physical life, and which millions of people across the world still believe to be the truth.

As in the telling of all other episodes throughout Jesus' life and ministry, the four canonical gospels differ in their narrative of the ending of Jesus' life. We must remember that these gospels are not, and were never intended to be, historical documents, hence the inaccurate historical information that permeates them all. The writers could not possibly have foreseen, over 2,000 years ago, that what they were writing then would become the basis, the fundamental teachings and dogmas of the world-wide church that came to be known as the Christian Church and the Roman Catholic Church. If they had known, then we could well speculate that they might have done a better job with their re-editing, copying and changing. What we actually have in the canonical gospels is sloppy re-editing, copying, interpolation and huge contradictions. They are theological writings, metaphoric and symbolic, not literal.

In my previous book 'And That's The Gospel Truth' I outlined in detail the discrepancies and contradictions in the four reports of the crucifixion, death and resurrection of Jesus, so there is no need to repeat all of that here. But there are further points and issues which must be raised and seriously questioned.

First, we must ask why was Jesus crucified? The emphasis here is on the word **crucified.** Not just killed. **Crucified!** That is an entirely different question from why was Jesus killed! And one which we must address.

So why was Jesus **crucified**?

Ask anyone to name two of the best known figures of the mid-twentieth century and the answer will probably be John F. Kennedy and Martin Luther King. Both men died from an assassin's bullet. Each was thought of as a hero. Both were followed and admired by millions. So why then did they die in that way, instead of living out their normal expected life span?

The answer?

Because someone, somewhere, wanted them dead. That's it in a nutshell! They both obviously had gone beyond the barriers and dictates of society. They had offended and angered some people.

So, in some people's opinion, they had to die.

Jesus too was followed and admired by many. Yet he was killed,- crucified, nailed to a cross, the most brutal and torturous form of punishment and execution imposed by Imperial Rome.

Why did Jesus die? The answer?

Again, simply because someone or some people wanted him dead. He had gone beyond the barriers and dictates of society. He had offended and angered some people. So, in some people's opinion, he had to die.

To understand Kennedy and King and what they were doing, or what they were attempting to do, we need to understand the society in which they lived. We need to understand the situation in post World War Two Europe and the World. We need to understand the Cold War mentality, where capitalist America and communist Russia, two opposing ideologies, faced one another across the Iron Curtain, each regarding the other with suspicion, distrust and above all, fear; the social, cultural and ethnic tensions of America in the 1960's; inequalities and discrimination; the ambitions of the Kennedy family themselves.

To help us understand all of this, we have ready access to a plethora of material. Many who were actually there on the spot and saw it all have given their evidence. Inquiry after Inquiry have given their verdict on who killed Kennedy. Conspiracy theories abound and still continue to circulate about government cover-ups, with sensationalist stories the subject of popular media and all genre of publications. Despite all of this, however, the truth is, we still do not know for certain who killed Kennedy!

And this is in our own life-time! Where media and modern technology bring us instant information at the press of a button, where we watch on our television screens as wars are fought out across the world, where everything is being investigated and questioned.

Similarly, if we are trying to understand Jesus, what he did and what he was trying to do, then we have to understand the times and place in which he lived. A much more difficult task than studying the life and times of Kennedy and King! No mass media, no mobile phones, no instant access to any kind of information, no watching on television as Jesus travels the land of Galilee in his ministry, no modern transport. Only a donkey, and the occasional camel caravan, laden with goods, travelling to and from the Mediterranean ports from Egypt, India and beyond. These were the news-bearers. And above all, no eye-witnesses. No first-hand accounts from people who were there at the time, telling us what they actually saw and heard.

Only writings handed down from hear-say, first written 30-70 years after the crucifixion; then the writings of historians such as Josephus, Tacitus, Pliny the Younger, followed by the writings of the early Church fathers.

So what do we generally know about the Crucifixion?

The Crucifixion of Jesus occurred in first-century Judea, most probably between the years 30 and 33 C.E.. It is described in the four canonical gospels, referred to in the New Testament epistles, attested to by other ancient sources, and is established as a historical event confirmed by non-Christian sources, although, among historians, there is no consensus on the precise details of what exactly occurred.

According to the canonical gospels, Jesus the Christ was arrested, tried and sentenced by Pontius Pilate to be scourged and finally crucified by the Romans. Jesus was stripped of his garments and offered wine mixed with gall to drink, before being crucified. He was then hung between two convicted thieves and according to Mark's Gospel, died some six hours later. During this time, the soldiers fixed a sign to the top of the cross stating '*Jesus of Nazareth, King of the Jews*' in three languages. They then divided his garments amongst themselves but cast lots for his seamless robe. After Jesus' death they pierced his side with a spear to be certain he was dead. The Bible describes several statements that Jesus made while he was on the cross, as well as several supernatural events that occurred.

So that's the story! All neatly packaged into the Nicene Creed, the outcome of the Council of Nicea in 325 C.E. at the instigation of the Emperor Constantine to bring some sort of order and cohesion to this new religion, this new religion designed to cement the Roman Empire together in a common bond of faith.

So let us start with the first fact. Jesus died because someone or some people wanted him dead. Therefore he must have done something to anger these people, whoever they were.

Indeed, according to the gospels, everyone except his disciples wanted Jesus dead. He certainly angered many sections of society. But! Unlike Kennedy or King, Jesus died not only because some people wanted him dead, but also because he himself freely chose to die! Jesus could have avoided the Roman authorities, and he could have stopped aggravating those same authorities if he had so wished!

So who were these people who wanted rid of him?

The mob apparently, according to the canonical gospels, wanted him dead. But that same mob, again according to the canonical gospels, that only a few days ago had welcomed him into Jerusalem with so much joy and enthusiasm. Jesus was tried in public before "*the Jews*", the crowds cried out that he should be crucified. Pilate then washed his hands of the matter. The gospels tell us that the Romans abdicated all responsibility for him.

The priestly Sadducees, representatives of the Jewish authorities, wanted him dead. Jesus had constantly challenged their authority. They saw Jesus as a threat to their power.

The Pharisees wanted him dead. He had constantly bickered and argued with them over the teachings in the Torah and of the Law.

Yes, Jesus had deliberately sought out the ruling religious and political authorities of his day, criticising them, antagonising them and making dangerous enemies of them.

But why *crucifixion*?

Crucifixion was historically the punishment for a political crime. According to the gospels, however, Pilate gave Jesus over to the mob, who then shouted for his crucifixion on the basis of religious dissent. Or so we are told!

But crucifixion was not the punishment for religious dissent. Stoning was!

Why would the Jewish mob call for crucifixion, a Roman punishment? They hated the Romans!

The Jewish execution for this particular transgression was death by stoning. Crucifixion was a Roman punishment reserved for sedition, not religious eccentricity. This contradiction alone illustrates that the gospels are not reporting the matter truthfully. Could they be trying to hide some vital aspects of the truth from us? Trying to blame the wrong people perhaps?

Jesus was, we can be certain, sentenced for execution on the basis of political crimes. We can also be certain that it was the Romans, not the Jewish authorities, who called the shots, whatever spin the gospels might try to put on it. And the gospels certainly spun the message that it was the mob who called for Jesus' crucifixion.

The crucial fact, however, remains uncontested that the fatal sentence was pronounced by the Roman governor and its execution carried out by Roman officials. It is certain that the movement connected with Jesus had at least some semblance of sedition to cause the Roman authorities both to regard him as a possible revolutionary and, after trial, to crucify him as guilty on such a charge.

So it is reasonable to conclude that Jesus was crucified for political reasons. Political reasons, not religious reasons. And what was the so-called crime involved? We can only conclude that the crime for which Jesus was crucified was sedition, and not the contravention of Jewish religious teachings.

Furthermore, Jesus was crucified between two other men, described as bandits in the gospels. However, if we go back to the original Greek text, they are described as '*lestes'*, brigands, the official name for Zealots, the Judaean freedom fighters who were dedicated to ridding Judaea of its Roman occupation.

"Then they crucified two bandits with Jesus, one on his right and the other on his left". (Matthew 27:38)

"They crucified Jesus there, and the two criminals". (Luke 23:32)

" One of the criminals hanging there hurled insults at him: 'Aren't you the Messiah? Save yourself and us!' " (Luke 23:39)

The Romans considered these men to be terrorists, Zealots. The

Zealots were not just concerned with the Romans, but also with the legitimacy of the priests serving in the Temple of Solomon and in particular, with the legitimacy of the high priest who was at the time, appointed by the Herodian rulers. They wanted priests who were *"sons of Aaron"*, priests of the bloodline of Aaron, the brother of Moses, of the tribe of Levi, who founded the Israelite priesthood and was the first high priest of Israel. *"The Sons of Aaron"* had become the sole legitimate line of priests in ancient Israel. And the Zealots were intent on keeping it that way!

The undeniable implication of Jesus' placement between two condemned Zealots at Golgotha is that, to the Roman authorities, Jesus also was a Zealot. As was Barabbas, the prisoner released under what is described as a feast-day amnesty by Pilate.

"At that time a man named Barabbas was in prison with the rebels who had committed murder in the riot". (Mark 14:6)

We know too that Jesus had Zealots amongst his disciples:

According to Matthew: *"These are the names of the twelve apostles: first, Simon, (called Peter), and his brother Andrew; James and his brother John the sons of Zebedee; Philip and Bartholomew; Thomas and Matthew the tax collector; James son of Alphaeus, and Thaddaeus; Simon the Patriot, and Judas Iscariot, who betrayed Jesus."* (Matthew 10:2-4)

"Simon, who was called the Patriot." (Luke 6:15)

Patriot was another name for Zealot. Zealots were so named because of their intense *'Zeal'* in opposing Roman rule. These Zealots had despised Herod for all that he represented. He was a Roman king, not a Jewish king and had become ruler of the Jews only through Roman help, boasting that he was *'the emperor's friend'*.

8

Then there were the '*Sacarii*', or dagger men, named after their '*sicae*', their sharp curved knives which they carried discretely hidden beneath the folds of their garments. The Sicarii carried out swift assassinations, disappearing quickly back into the crowd again. They were always on the alert and ready to seize any opportune moment to assassinate any Roman official or supporter. Judas '*Iscariot*' has strong connotations of the word '*sicarii'*, and indeed was known to have been one of them.

"But now," Jesus said, 'whoever has a purse or a bag must take it, and whoever has no sword must sell his coat and buy one. For I tell you that the scripture which says 'He shared the fate of criminals', must come true about me, because what was written about me is coming true.'

The disciples said, 'Look! Here are two swords, Lord!

'That is enough!' he replied."   (Luke 22: 36-38)

"When the disciples who were with Jesus saw what was going to happen, they asked, 'Shall we use our swords, Lord?' And one of them struck the High Priest's slave, and cut off his right ear." (Luke 22:49-50)

"Simon Peter, who had a sword, drew it and struck the High Priest's slave, cutting off his right ear. The name of the slave was Malchus. Jesus said to Peter, 'Put your sword back in its place! Do you think that I will not drink the cup of suffering which my Father has given me?" (John 18:10-11)

"One of those who were with Jesus drew his sword and struck at the High Priest's slave, cutting off his ear". (Matthew 26:51)

Thanks to John, we now know who it was who cut off the ear!

"Simon Peter, who had a sword, drew it and struck the High Priest's

slave, cutting off his right ear." (John 18:10)

Simon Peter!

Now we must ask the question, if Jesus was preaching peace, what was Peter doing carrying a sword?

And Peter was not the only one carrying a sword!

"Shall we use our swords Lord?" (Luke 22:50

Jesus certainly was surrounded by violent men!

But apart from whether or not Jesus was crucified as a Zealot or insurgent, there is another unavoidable issue here.

The prophecies!

"These are the very things I told you about while I was still with you: everything written about me in the Law of Moses, the writings of the prophets, and the Psalms had to come true............This is what was written: The messiah must suffer and must rise from death three days later, and in his name the message about repentance and the forgiveness of sins must be preached to all nations, beginning in Jerusalem". (Luke: 24:44-47)

So Jesus had to rise from the dead. First, though, before he could rise from the dead, he had to get himself killed. And as we have seen, not just killed! Not stoned! Not burned!

Jesus had to specifically get himself ***crucified!***

Crucifixion is specifically mentioned in the gospel of Matthew:

" 'Listen,' he told them, 'we are going up to Jerusalem, where the Son of Man will be handed over to the chief priests and the teachers of the Law. They will condemn him to death and then hand him over to the Gentiles, who will mock him, whip him, and

crucify him, but three days later he will be raised to life.' "
(Matthew 20:18-19)

We need look no further than Psalm 22 for the foreshadowing of the Crucifixion. Matthew and Mark both tell us that the words of Jesus on the cross were*: 'My God, my God, why have you forsaken me?'* These words, however, are actually the first line of Psalm 22, written by King David, 1000 years previously:

 "My God, my God, why have you abandoned me?"

So Jesus had to be **crucified**! The prophecies foretold it! And those same prophecies had to be fulfilled. And Jesus knew it!

And the trumped-up charge? Desecrating the Temple and destroying the Jewish religious beliefs!

But the real charge?

Jesus died by crucifixion. Crucifixion was a Roman punishment. Jesus was not a Roman. Crucifixion was for perdition, sedition or political disturbances. Jesus had been accused of religious offences! He was crucified between two brigands, or Zealots, and the title '*King of the Jews*' was inscribed above the cross.

So we must ask, was Jesus a Zealot?

Was Jesus really the mild, meek and docile person depicted in the gospels?

He himself admitted:

"No one is good except God." (Mark 10:18)

And why did no one try to save Jesus? His disciples all ran away! The Zealots could certainly have saved him! They had the physical power! So why did they allow him to be crucified?

11

Were the Zealots angry with Jesus because he had let them down by not leading an armed uprising? Or because he had told the people to pay their taxes to Caesar?

And did Judas betray Jesus at the last moment in a desperate attempt to draw him out and proclaim an uprising? Then, when Jesus did not respond, was that why Judas then took his own life? Because he realised Jesus was not a violent revolutionary and he, Judas had just condemned the wrong man?

There are certainly lots of unanswered questions surrounding Jesus' **Crucifixion**!

Furthermore, we must consider Jesus' entry into Jerusalem on what is known as Palm Sunday. Jesus made a flamboyant, an elaborate, a big entry into the city, surrounded by cheering, embracing crowds, who threw palm branches down in front of him as he rode in, as the scriptures foretold, on a donkey.

Now this was a Jesus who had spent the whole three years of his public ministry avoiding large cities, travelling around the smaller villages and communities in the Galilee area. He avoided the larger cities, especially Jerusalem because he knew his life was in danger from the authorities, against whom he had been preaching, holding them up for ridicule and admonishment each and every chance he got. He openly argued with the Pharisees and the Sadducees as well as the priests of the Temple.

Now, here he was, entering Jerusalem in a very public way! And then what does he proceed to do? He wrecks the stalls in the Temple! Talk about making yourself the centre of attention! And the place swarming with Roman soldiers drafted in specially to maintain order during the politically sensitive feast of the Passover! His disciples certainly feared for his safety, and did not want him to return to Jerusalem, but the gospels do not tell us why. Jesus was safe when he was in the Galilee or Capernaum area, Philip's domain, where he was beyond the power of the Jerusalem authorities.

BUT! The strange thing is that the Roman soldiers watching all this turned a blind eye to the actions of Jesus! Those Roman soldiers positioned around the vast Temple complex with the purpose of maintaining order when the Temple and Jerusalem swarmed with Jews from across all the Mediterranean area and the known world.

So why was Jesus not arrested when he broke up the Temple stalls, starting a riot? Why was he not arrested until a few days later, in the dark of night in the Garden of Gethsemane?

There can only be one answer! Jesus was obviously being protected by someone high up in political circles! But who? Someone who had an interest in allowing Jesus to wreck the Temple stalls and go against the priests of the Temple!

Protected by whom? Protected by Pontius Pilate? Could that be in any way possible? Political intrigue?

It is well recorded that there was no love lost between Pilate and the Jewish religious and political authorities. They regarded him as weak and he knew it! It was his repeated insensitivity towards Jewish customs and beliefs that apparently caused his removal from office in 36 C.E., by the Syrian governor, Vitellius, and ordered to Rome to face charges of excessive cruelty. Josephus tells us that Pilate outraged the Jews by several tactless, insensitive actions, such as using the temple funds to build an aqueduct and introducing military standards and flags bearing the emperor's image, all of which seriously offended Jewish religious traditions.

Let us now look at something else Josephus wrote! Josephus refers to Jesus only twice by that name in all his writings, and many scholars believe one was an interpolation, the famous *'Testamonium Flavium'*, leading many to conclude that Jesus therefore did not exist. But Josephus did speak a lot about Jesus! Where? Under the name *'Wonderworker'* as in the following:

"And there assembled unto him of ministers one hundred and fifty, and a multitude of the people. Now when they saw his power, that he accomplished whatsoever he would by a word, and when they had made known to him their will, that he should enter into the city and cut down the Roman troops and Pilate and rule over us, but he took no notice. And when therefore knowledge of it came to the Jewish leaders, they assembled together with the high priest and spake: 'We are powerless and too weak to withstand the Romans. Seeing moreover that the bow is bent, we will go and communicate with Pilate what we have heard, and we shall be clear of trouble.' And Pilate had that **Wonderworker** *brought up, and after instituting an inquiry concerning him, he pronounced judgement: 'He is a benefactor, not a malefactor, nor a rebel, nor covetous of kingship.' And he let him go, for he had healed his dying wife. And he went to his wonted place and did his wonted works. And when more people again assembled round him, he glorified himself through his actions more than all. The teachers of the Law were overcome with envy, and* **gave thirty talents to Pilate**, *in order that he should put him to death.* **And he took it and gave them liberty to execute their will themselves.** *And they laid hands on him and crucified him* **contrary to the law of their fathers**."

So what are we to make of all this?

It all certainly smacks of political intrigue! And political intrigue at the highest levels! Did the Jewish authorities crucify Jesus, using the Roman form of execution, having bribed Pilate for permission to do so? And remember, they had arrested Jesus in the dark of night in the Garden of Gethsemane, and not in broad daylight!

Alternatively, did the Roman authorities condemn Jesus to death, using the jeering Jewish mob as the scapegoat? The canonical gospels certainly go to great lengths to exonerate Pilate from any part in Jesus' death! But of course they would! They were written as Roman propaganda!

In a letter from Pontius Pilate to the Roman Emperor Tiberius Caesar, concerning Jesus, we read:

"Unwilling to interrupt Him (Jesus) by my presence, I continued my walk but signified to my secretary to join their group and listen. Later, my secretary reported that never had he seen in the works of all the philosophers anything that compared to the teachings of Jesus. He told me that Jesus was neither seditious nor rebellious, so we extended to Him our protection. He was at liberty to act, to speak, to assemble and to address the people. This unlimited freedom provoked the Jews---not the poor but the rich and powerful."

So here we see Pilate offering Jesus protection!

Will we ever get the truth? Will we ever know the full story? Conspiracy theories abound concerning the Crucifixion of Jesus as much as those concerning the assassination of President Kennedy.

But! It is vitally important to keep asking the questions!

And of course, we must continue to question that crowd that greeted Jesus with so much enthusiasm only to turn so violently against him just four days later. Just four days? What could have happened during just those four days to explain such a change?

Many scholars are now putting forward the theory that what the gospels relate as happening in Holy Week could not possibly have happened within such a short space of time. Those palm branches which were strewn in front of Jesus are even in question! September to October, the time of the Jewish Feast of Tabernacles was the time for palm branches, not April! This feast celebrated the gathering in of the harvest. So this means that Jesus must have entered Jerusalem in late September or October, six months prior to the time specified in the gospels. Those six months, unaccounted for in the gospels, would certainly have been sufficient time for the crowd to turn against Jesus. Why? Well, when Jesus entered Jerusalem they saw him as the Messiah, the one who was going to deliver them from the oppression of Roman rule, the one who would drive the Romans out of their land.

But as time progressed it was obvious Jesus was not going to start an insurrection, hence the cheering crowd changed to a jeering crowd, calling for his crucifixion. Six months was sufficient time for them to realise that Jesus was not what they had taken him to be. And hence, as we have already seen, the change of attitude on the part of Judas Iscariot.

We will be returning to the Crucifixion of Jesus at the end of this book, when we pose the question **DID JESUS REALLY DIE ON THE CROSS?**

But now we must consider how Jesus has been lost for the last 2,000 years.

PART TWO: JESUS LOST

CHAPTER 2

The New Testament Writings And Jesus

Contrary to what millions of people across the world still believe, the canonical gospels and the Acts of the Apostles were not written by the disciples, or even by any contemporaries of Jesus. These writings are all included in the New Testament, which in turn is part of the Bible, proclaimed as, and believed by millions, to be the 'divinely inspired word of God', the 'holy book' of the Christian Church. In fact, we do not even know who the writers were. They were written under pseudo names, which was usual for that time. And the order in which they were written has always been misrepresented to us by orthodox religion. Nor do we have four independent accounts of the life of Jesus, contrary to what the church has argued for the last 2,000 years. Mark, written first, was copied freely by Matthew and Luke. Then John gives us a different account.

Indeed, if His Divine Self was the inspiration behind the Bible writings, then His Divine Self must have often been very confused and must have had a lot of off-days! Why? Simply because the gospels are permeated with contradictions, exaggerations, historical inaccuracies, distortions, interpolations, story-telling, copying, and sloppy re-editing.

So let us get it right!

The New Testament writings are not and never were intended to be historical documents. They are theological documents.

Theological documents first written several decades after the supposed death of Jesus. The information contained in them had been passed down orally for all those years before someone began to write it all down. Those writers, whoever they were, could not possibly have foreseen that their writings would come to form the basis of the newly fledged Christian Church 300 years later and still be the main teachings 2,000 years later!

We have always been led to believe that the canonical gospels, Matthew, Mark, Luke and John were written first, and in that particular order, followed by the Acts of the Apostles. However, if we look at the date of each of these writings, we get a very different story.

In order of date, we have, first Paul's letters, written 50-60 C.E. Then we have the Gospel of Mark, 70 C.E., then Matthew, 80-85 C.E., then Luke, 85-90 C.E., and then John, 90-100 C.E. Finally, we have the Acts, a continuation of the Gospel of Luke and written by the same author. Paul himself was beheaded by the Romans in 67 C.E. during the reign of Nero, so we can see that all of the four Gospels were written after his death. We can clearly see that all four gospel writers had Paul's letters before them when they wrote their gospels. Paul was the self-proclaimed apostle, arriving on the scene only after the alleged death of Jesus. He never knew or met Jesus, but proclaimed that his knowledge came from a series of visions and appearances made to him by Jesus after the alleged resurrection. So Paul's beliefs would have been known to the writers of the gospels.

So why have we always been presented with a different order? Obviously to cover up the fact that the gospel writers would have been heavily influenced by the writings of Paul! Paul, whose writings came to be the basis of church teachings, doctrines and dogmas! Paul, who deified and mythologised Jesus, competing with other Roman and Greek gods of the time, all of whom were born of virgins, died and resurrected. Paul, who established Jesus as a sacrificial figure, dying for the sins of all mankind! Paul, who taught that faith and faith alone would bring redemption. Faith! The foundation stone on which the Christian church is built!

All of these writings are included in the New Testament, and the first person to list the Christian Canon of the New Testament was the Church father Athanasius, in the year 367 C.E. Earlier, toward the end of the first century, church theologians had begun to monitor the teachings of the various groups with a view to bringing them all under one central governing body. Bishop Irenaeus of Lyons set out a canon in which the Jewish scriptures were named as the Old Testament. Now Athanasius, as Bishop of Alexandria, the same Athanasius who had starred so prominently at the Council of Nicea in 325 C.E., convened by the Emperor Constantine to bring some sort of order and cohesion into the new fledgling church, issued his 39th Festal Letter:

"......I must without hesitation mention the scriptures of the New Testament; they are the following: the four Gospels according to Matthew, Mark, Luke and John, and after them the Acts of the Apostles, and the seven so-called catholic epistles of the apostles, namely, one of James, two of Peter, then three of John and after these one of Jude. In addition, there are fourteen epistles of the apostle Paul written in the following order: the first to the Romans, then two to the Corinthians and then after these the one to the Galatians, following it the one to the Ephesians, thereafter the one to the Philippians, and the one to the Colossians and two to the Thessalonians and the epistle to the Hebrews and then immediately two to Timothy, one to Titus and lastly the one to

Philemon............These are the springs of salvation, in order that he who is thirsty may fully refresh himself with the words contained in them. In them alone is the doctrine of piety proclaimed. Let no one add anything to them or take away anything from them..... "

It was this list of works that was ratified at both the Council of Hippo in 393 C.E. and at the Council of Carthage in 397 C.E. Their content was somewhat altered, however, to reflect church policy. All other writings, viewpoints and opinions about Jesus and Christian doctrine would be considered heresy and punishable by persecution and death. They became a tool, but a powerful tool, in the hands of the Christian Church.

So how come so many of us have managed to miss all this?

Well, firstly, we have never actually been encouraged to read the gospels for ourselves. What most of us know from the gospels has been from our compulsory, under-pain-of-sin-and-hence-punishment attendance at church on Sunday mornings, captive audiences where the so-called word of God was thundered out at us from the pulpit.

Secondly, those who did have sufficient interest to read the writings of the New Testament for themselves, probably read the four gospels vertically and consecutively, one after the other, from beginning to end, in the exact order they have been presented to us, Matthew first, beginning with the birth of Jesus, then Mark, then Luke and finally John. Reading the gospels vertically, one does not see the inaccuracies, the disunity, the contradictions which permeate them. One tends to see the general story, wrapped in unity and harmony. However, if read horizontally, and comparatively, then what hits the reader sharply in the face is the lack of unity and harmony, the lack of agreement, the lack of similarity. Discrepancies and differences abound, leaping out from the pages, forcing the reader to reflect on what has been handed down to us through history as the '*divinely inspired word of God*'. But we are forced to ask, which parts are inspired and which parts are not? One thing is certain. It can't all be inspired!

Every writer, every literary script, reflects in some way the society in which the writer lived. Charles Dickens reflects Dickensian society, telling us more about that society, more about its poverty and corrupt moral values than any history book could do. Likewise the novels of Jane Austen depict, through satire, the societal foibles of her era. And the New Testament writings are no different. They were written in first-century Jewish Palestine, and whilst not being in any way historical documents, they do reflect to a large extent the society of first-century Jewish Judea and Galilee. We will see in greater detail in a later chapter how first-century Palestine was not a peaceful place. Conflict permeated every aspect of Jewish life. And this is indeed reflected, this is indeed mirrored in the gospels.

Everyone in the gospels is at everyone else's throat. As already noted, the New Testament is supposed to be the '*holy book*' of the Christian Church! The "*divinely inspired word of God*"! So how come it is so full to bursting with hatred, animosity, dissent, political and religious wrangling, discrimination, quarrelling, derision, conflict and violence?

Jesus is the hero, the main performer, center stage, the star of the whole show, permeating everything and everywhere.

But Jesus is at loggerheads with everyone! He castigates the Pharisees; he openly derides the Sadducees; he clearly hates and scorns the high priests and the entire Temple system; he shows scorn and contempt for the Law. They in turn fight constantly with him, trying to catch him out and accusing him of breaking the Law, even trying to kill him. And of course, how can we possibly forget! Jesus angrily wrecked the stalls in the Temple complex! Accompanied by the most offensive name-calling!

Then we have the on-going conflict between the Pharisees and the Sadducees. The Pharisees hate the Sadducees, who in turn have no love for the Pharisees. Constant bickering, arguing, accusing, name-calling! And no one likes the Samaritans, considering them impure and the lowliest of all the many fractious sects. No one even talks to them! Remember how Jesus' disciples upbraided him for simply talking to the Samaritan woman at the well?

The disciples fight and argue amongst themselves, each vying and lobbying for position and reward. The male disciples hate the female disciples. After Jesus' death, we see in the Acts of the Apostles the huge differences between the followers of James, the brother of Jesus, and the followers of Paul. There is open conflict. Peter openly rebukes Paul for deviating from the teachings of Jesus. Peter says Paul is wrong. Paul says Peter is wrong. Paul says he knows more than the disciples of Jesus know, because so much has been revealed to him in visions of the risen Jesus. James, the brother of Jesus, who took over the leadership of the Jesus movement after the death of Jesus, declares that good works are the most important for salvation. Paul openly and forcefully disagrees. He teaches that only faith can guarantee salvation. Then the disciples send Paul away to teach to the Gentiles. Followers of each side want to kill followers of the other side.

Then we have the prevalence of the carrying of knives and swords. The ear of the high priest's servant is cut off by Peter in the Garden of Gethsemane when Jesus is arrested. There is an infiltration of

Zealots and Sicarii within the Jesus ranks, those who resorted to violent means and advocated violent uprisings and assassinations as the only means of ending the oppressive Roman rule. They despised and hated anyone who dared to pay their taxes to the Romans.

Everyone is at loggerheads with everyone else! All are villains, disturbers of the peace.

Except! Except of course the Romans! The Romans come out smelling of roses! They are the good guys in this complex story. Even exonerated from the Crucifixion of Jesus. The Jews are made the scape-goats!

Let us re-iterate Leonardo da Vinci's words again!

"O wretched mortals! Open your eyes!"

We need to open our eyes to the truth about the writings in the New Testament! They are man-written, not God-written! They were written by men for a very specific purpose! To deify and mythologise Jesus! To compete with the other gods of the time! All born of virgins, all raised from the dead!

And all solidified into a convenient, coherent, wholesome package to serve the needs of the expanding Roman Empire. All given substance and credence by the Roman Emperor Constantine, who convened the Council of Nicaea in 325 C.E. specifically to establish allegiance and unity out of the diversity of the ethnic populations and the diverse beliefs composing the Roman Empire. Constantine who professed to be a Christian while at the same time continuing to pay homage to the gods of the Roman Empire. Religion of convenience! And all this after 300 years of persecution of the Christians! Christianity declared legal and desirable in the Roman

Empire in 321 C.E. when Constantine saw how advantageous the presence of Christian churches would be to him! Christianity now proclaimed as the one and only religion of the entire Roman Empire! And after 300 years of the most brutal persecution! How ironic is that!

"O wretched mortals! Open your eyes!"

We need to open our eyes to the truth of the Jesus created by the New Testament writings, the truth about Jesus the created god-man, created to compete with other gods of his time, like Osiris, Dionysius, Mithras, all born of virgins, all dying and resurrecting.

The New Testament writings are nothing more than spin, Roman spin! Extremist propaganda! Eccentric brain-washing!

And you know what is the greatest irony in all of this?

The fact that the Christian Church itself has selected only various parts of the New Testament writings for promulgation! Inconvenient bits have been left out, as if they never existed. Selective truths! Selective evidencing! They keep repeating all the good bits about Jesus, nothing negative, nothing derogative! All about Jesus the god! But what about Jesus the man?

Those early church fathers who selected these particular gospels were not interested in Jesus the man. They were only interested in Jesus the god. The fountain head of their new church!

According to Acts, Jesus' twelve disciples were instrumental in spreading his teachings and the Christian religion after his death. Yes, they may well have spread the teachings of Jesus after his death, but they certainly did not spread Christianity! And why not? Because Jesus was not a Christian! Jesus was a Jew! Jesus was a human being, a man, made of flesh and blood, like all humans. Not a deified man! A real flesh and blood man! And his disciples did not see Jesus as a deity! Jesus' early followers saw him as the Messiah, a human King of the House of David, who was going to save Israel from Roman rule. The use of the word *Christian* itself was first recorded in the New Testament, after Barnabas brought Paul to Antioch where they taught "*a large group*" for about a year:

"It was at Antioch that the believers were first called Christians." (Acts 11:26)

In fact, much of the mythology of Christianity is simply a re-do of the older and more transparent beliefs of Judaism!

Is it not amazing that millions of church goers around the world continue to profess belief in the New Testament writings without ever having even read them? It is like going to a course and not reading the manual! Going into an exam without having read the prescribed text!

Is it not amazing that millions of church goers around the world still profess allegiance to an institution that has the greatest of all criminal records?

Is it not amazing that millions of church goers around the world still fail to see the untold mental, emotional and physical damage inflicted on countless lives by the puritanical, hypocritical, barbaric methods used as the centuries have passed, by a Church that professes to be the one and only true Church, the Church of Christ?

Is it not amazing that millions of church goers around the world still believe that the Christian Church has always been open about its teachings? The very idea of secret gospels, with teachings deliberately kept hidden from public consumption, is still deeply unacceptable to the average Christian.

Is it not amazing that millions of church goers around the world still believe that everything related in the gospels is true? Continuing to turn a blind eye to all the inconsistencies, all the contradictions, all the spin?

But if we put these gospels under the microscope, we will find a very different story! So let us do just that! Let us put these gospels under the microscope and see what we will find!

"Many people have done their best to write a report of the things that have taken place among us. They wrote what we have been told by those who saw these things from the beginning and who proclaimed the message." (Luke 1:1-2)

Who were these "*many people*" to whom Luke was referring in his opening lines?

"Now, there are many other things that Jesus did. If they were all written down one by one, I suppose that the whole world could not hold the books that would be written." (John 21:25)

So obviously, a lot more happened than we have been told!

First and foremost, Jesus was a teacher.

"Jesus went all over Galilee, teaching in the synagogues, preaching the Good News about the Kingdom." (Matthew 4:23)

"He taught in the synagogues and was praised by everyone." (Luke 4:15)

Yes, he was also a healer and a miracle worker, but most of his mission was given over to teaching. It was his teachings that astounded the people. They had never heard anything like this before. And it was his teachings that got him into trouble with the authorities, with the Pharisees and with the Sadducees.

Yet, despite all this, we are not told in the canonical gospels a great amount of what Jesus actually taught! Yes, we are constantly told that he taught, but we are not always told **what** he taught. He spent hours at a time preaching to the crowd, days even, but we are not told what he actually said! For example, at the feeding of the four thousand:

"Jesus called the disciples to him and said, 'I feel sorry for these people, because they have been with me for three days and now have nothing to eat. If I send them home without feeding them, they will faint as they go, because some of them have come a long way.' " (Mark 8:2-3)

And at the miracle of the loaves and fishes:

"When the sun was beginning to set, the twelve disciples came to him and said, 'Send the people away so that they can go to the villages and farms round here and find food and lodging, because this is a lonely place.' " (Luke 9:12)

Now, if he could keep the crowd listening to him for such long periods of time, three days even, and they had followed him to a remote area, then he must have been saying something of interest!

But why are we not told what Jesus preached to the crowd?

Why are there no writings of Jesus? Because he was illiterate? Hardly!

The one occasion in the gospels when he did write is shrouded in mystery!

"The teachers of the Law and the Pharisees brought in a woman who had been caught committing adultery, and they made her stand before them all. 'Teacher', they said to Jesus, 'this woman was caught in the very act of committing adultery. In our Law Moses commanded that such a woman must be stoned to death. Now, what do you say?' They said this to trap Jesus, so that they could accuse him. But he bent over and wrote on the ground with his finger.

As they stood there asking him questions, he straightened himself up and said to them, 'Whichever one of you has committed no sin may throw the first stone at her.' Then he bent over again and wrote on the ground. When they heard this, they all left, one by one, the older ones first." (John 8:3-9)

So what did Jesus write in the dust? Did he write the names of those particular Pharisees who had sinned the most? And the name of the sin they had committed? Or perhaps he just wrote the word *'Forgiven'*? Or perhaps he just drew a symbol? We are not told!

But whatever it was, it certainly cleared the place very quickly, as they all took off!

And Jesus could read:

"Then Jesus went to Nazareth, where he had been brought up, and on the Sabbath he went as usual to the synagogue. He stood up to read the Scriptures and was handed the book of the prophet Isaiah. He unrolled the scroll and found the place where it is written: 'The Spirit of the Lord is upon me..........' Jesus rolled up the scroll, gave it back to the attendant, and sat down." (Luke 4: 16-20)

The gospels are permeated with examples of Jesus being very cognisant of the prophecies and the writings in the Old Testament, and, as we shall see in a later chapter, he was constantly referring to the prophecies being fulfilled.

So if Jesus was literate, then why did he not leave any writings for posterity?

And if he knew, as we shall also see, that he was going to fulfil so many of the prophecies himself, then is it not logical to assume that he would have left some writings?

There are many occasions throughout the canonical gospels where there are obvious gaps, all to do with the teachings of Jesus. For example, after the Resurrection, when Jesus appeared to his disciples on the road to Emmaus:

"And Jesus explained to them what was said about himself in all the Scriptures, beginning with the book of Moses and going through all the prophets." (Luke 24:27)

That was certainly, by any standards, a very long explanation!

But that's it! That's all we are told! Not one word of what he said!

Huge gaps such as this appear throughout the gospels!

"They came to Jericho, and as Jesus was leaving with his disciples and a large crowd........" (Mark 10:46)

What happened in Jericho? We are not told!

"While Jesus was having a meal in Matthew's house, many tax collectors and other outcasts came and joined Jesus and his disciples at the table. Some Pharisees saw this and asked his disciples, 'Why does your teacher eat with such people?' "

(Matthew 90:10-11)

What was said? We are not told! Or did they all eat in silence? Hardly!

"Then Jesus left and went away to the territory near the city of Tyre. He went into a house and did not want anyone to know he was there, but he could not stay hidden." (Mark 7:24)

Whose house was it? We are not told!

So, obviously a lot of information has been kept from us!

Including the intriguing relationship between Jesus and Lazarus and his sisters Martha and Mary!

"The sisters sent Jesus a message: 'Lord, your dear friend is ill.' " (John 11:3)

Jesus we are told, often took refuge in the house of Lazarus, communing with the family. But what was said? What was the nature of their friendship? How did they become friends? What exactly went on in Bethany? What significance did the family at Bethany have in the life and mission of Jesus?

Again, we are not told!

"The guards answered, 'Nobody has ever talked like this man.' " (John 7:46)

Like what exactly? We are not told! And these were the guards, sent to keep an eye on Jesus! Even Jesus' instructions to his disciples as to what to preach:

"Then he sent them out to preach the Kingdom of God and to heal the sick..........The disciples left and travelled through all the villages, preaching the Good News and healing people

everywhere." (Luke 9:2-6)

But what exactly were those instructions? We are not told!

And what were his instructions to them just before he ascended to heaven?

"All authority in heaven and on earth has been given to Me. Therefore, go and make disciples in all actions, baptizing them in the name of the Father, and of the Son, and of the Holy Spirit; Teaching them to observe **ALL** *things that I have commanded you. And lo, I am with you always, even until the end of the age."* (Matthew 28:18-20)

So what were ALL these things that he had commanded them to teach? We are not told!

And when Jesus spoke to them about the *"things pertaining to heaven",* what was that all about? We are never told!

"Jesus preached his messages to the people, using many other parables like these; he told them as much as they could understand. He would not speak to them without using parables, but when he was alone with his disciples, he would explain everything to them." (Mark 4:33-34)

"Then the disciples came to Jesus and asked him, 'Why do you use parables when you talk to the people?'

Jesus answered. 'The knowledge about the secrets of the Kingdom of heaven has been given to you, but not to them. For the person who has something will be given more, so that he will have more than enough; but the person who has nothing will have taken away from him even the little he has. The reason I use parables in talking to them is that they look, but do not see, and they listen, but do not hear.' " (Matthew 13:10-13)

But again, we are not told what Jesus explained to his disciples in private! We are told the parables, but not the secret teachings to the inner circle!

And, of course, the greatest gap of all!

The missing years from Jesus was twelve years old until he was thirty and at the start of his ministry! Eighteen years sure is a big gap!

So it is very reasonable to assume from all of this that the New Testament writings are very restricted and do not give us much. It is also reasonable to assume that the early church fathers had access to a plethora of other material!

So what is all this other material? Where is all this other material?

And what about all the correspondence and communication going to and fro in the newly founded Church at Jerusalem, the Church headed by James the brother of Jesus? Yes, we get information in the Acts of the Apostles, in the writings of Paul about the rift that occurred between himself and James, when James and Peter summoned Paul to Jerusalem to face charges that he was not teaching the true teachings of Jesus. But where is the correspondence between Peter and James or between both of these to the other members of that church, the mother church of the Christian faith?

We are told in the gospels that Jesus sent out 72 others.

"After this the Lord chose another 72 men and sent them out two by two to go ahead of him to every town and place where he himself was about to go." (Luke 10:1)

So where did these appear from? Who were they? We are not told!

And yes, he gave them specific instructions about what to take and what not to take with them and what to do when they were welcomed or not welcomed. But we are not told what he instructed them to teach!

Not only Jesus' teachings are shrouded in mystery by the canonical gospels, but so too is much of his healing.

Very often, Jesus took the sick man quietly aside away from the public gaze. Other times he took only his closest disciples into the room with him. And on several occasions he ordered the cured man to keep his cure secret.

So we are left with the same question! What happened to all the other material that we can logically and realistically assume was written at that time?

One possibility was that a lot of it might have perished with the destruction of Jerusalem in 70 C.E. And remember, the canonical gospels were written after that time!

And another possibility?

The burning of the library at Alexandria!

The Ancient Library of Alexandria in Egypt was one of the largest and most significant libraries of the ancient world. It flourished as a center of learning and scholarship from its construction in the 3rd century B.C.E. until the Roman conquest of Egypt in 30 B.C.E. The library itself was part of a larger establishment, the Museum of Alexandria, where many of the most famous literary men, philosophers and thinkers of the ancient world studied. Ironically, though, it is most famous because of its burning! Countless papyrus scrolls, manuscripts and books were destroyed, and its destruction has become a symbol for the loss of cultural knowledge. Sources differ on who exactly was responsible for its destruction, but possible theories include a fire set by the army of Julius Caesar in 48 B.C.E. when he found himself surrounded by Egyptian forces in Alexandria, and an attack by the Emperor Aurelian 270-275 C.E. during an uprising against Rome by Queen Zenobia of Palmyra.

This library at Alexandria may very well have contained many of the precious books and writings which we are missing today. Writings by Jesus may well have been amongst them!

But the most likely possibility of all?

The widespread burnings and spate of destruction unleashed by the early church fathers after they decided which writings would constitute the four canonical gospels and the other writings in the New Testament. All other material was declared heretic and consigned to the flames.

So those who wrote the alternative material had only one choice! To hide it!

And a lot of that hidden material has been found! Found buried in caves and under the desert in Egypt! In places like Nag Hammadi!

But it is now time for us to look at how Jesus the man was buried by the early Christian Church and how and why the Jesus of faith was created by that same church.

CHAPTER 3

JESUS BURIED BY THE EARLY CHRISTIAN CHURCH

Every year, countless numbers of tourists make their way to the Holy Land, expecting to walk the paths that they believe Jesus walked with his disciples. Guided by enthusiastic, but misguided tour guides, they are ushered through and around all the sites known and recognisable by their Biblical place names, - Jerusalem; Bethlehem; Sea of Galilee; the Dead Sea; Garden of Gethsemane; Nazareth. Awe-inspiring, to say the least!

When I first visited the Holy Land in 1984, I too stood in awe, taking in all the guides were saying. I too truly believed I was walking in the footsteps of Jesus.

Now I know better!

Now I know that the same ground upon which Jesus walked no longer exists. Now I know that most places associated with Jesus have been buried over time, many feet below ground level, modern buildings standing where historic Biblical buildings are reputed to have once stood 2,000 years ago.

Now I know that absolutely nothing has been preserved. And why not? Obviously because no-one could have foreseen the impact Christianity would come to have on succeeding generations. Any preservation that has taken place, any buildings that have been erected, any areas designated as Biblical, have only been on the *supposed* sites, and sold to devout pilgrims as the *real* thing, the *real* place where Jesus was born, the *real* places where he preached and taught, the *real* place where he died and the *real* place where he was buried.

Jerusalem has passed through numerous phases in the last 2,000 years, of occupation by different cultures and civilisations, alterations, demolitions and re-constructions. New buildings have been constructed over old buildings in constant succession so much so that the streets you now walk are about one hundred feet above the original level. Between your footsteps and the spots where Jesus walked, lie tons and tons of debris and rubble, all forming the foundations for the modern buildings.

This small stretch of land on the south east coast of the Mediterranean is only approximately 100 miles by 150 miles. In ancient times, this land was called Canaan. In Jesus' time, it was called Judah, renamed Judea by the Romans, after they occupied that territory. Now it is known as Israel and Palestine. For the Jewish people, it is still the Promised Land; for Christians, it is the Holy Land. Jews themselves take their name from Judaea, the Greek version of Judah, the southern part, and their religion was Judaism. All three monotheistic faiths - Jews, Christians and Muslims, have claimed ownership and allegiance to this land. For Jews and Christians, Jerusalem is recognised as the Holy City; for Muslims, Jerusalem is second only to Mecca and Medina.

Jerusalem was important in ancient times because it was easy to defend, being on a hilltop, with houses built on the steep slopes and accessed through steep steps on different levels. It also had natural water springs flowing freely under it. Underground reservoirs ensured a constant supply of water, connected by pipes and conduits. The Romans, after all, were famous for their public works and irrigation systems!

Jerusalem itself was often called by its synonym, Zion, after its citadel, and became the focus and subject of patriotic songs for both Jews and Christians. It has been immortalised in the words of the song:

'By the rivers of Babylon, there we sat down. Yeah, we remember Zion'. (Psalm 137:1) (Samuel 2: 5:7, about 630-540 BCE)

Now here is a question for thought!

Can you name one country, just one country, that ever benefitted from the coming of Christianity? That same Christianity that down through the centuries has claimed to bring civilization to so-called pagan countries!

And what exactly does the word pagan imply?

Our early ancestors were pagans, their way of life very different from ours. They had a deep affinity with Nature in that they not only knew Nature, but they also controlled Nature. Through the sounds and subtle energies of Nature, and the subtle energies and the power of the light of the heavenly bodies, they understood the secrets of life and of creation. They saw, heard and felt the messages constantly being brought to them through Nature. To them, Nature was God, and through their connection with Mother Nature they had access to a Spirituality that enabled them to live in a joyful, peaceful and harmonious way.

Paganism was not a religion. It transcended all that religious stuff that we fill our minds with today. It was a culture, a way of life, the greatest, the most marvellous culture alive on earth, belonging to a very highly Spiritual civilisation. They understood the purpose of each and every form of life, every blade of grass, every leaf, every insect and animal, every plant and planet. They understood the inter-connection between all forms of life and they respected that inter-connection. They understood the Oneness of the All, the meaning and the working of energy, and how energy can be used for the good of mankind.

Today, the religion of Japan, the native religion of SHINTOISM, is the closest we have to paganism. The word SHINTO translates to pathway of the Gods. According to Shinto, Man's ultimate goal is harmonious co-existence with Nature. But under the influence of the Christian Church over centuries, the term pagan has acquired a strong negative connotation. At the same time, the word Christian has also become a word-symbol. But it symbolises, by contrast, spirituality, decency, enlightened thought, closeness to God. Pagan, on the other hand, has come to mean foul, vile, unclean. People now think of pagans as terrible and uncivilised.

Nothing could be further from the truth!

Yes! Christianity has desecrated the whole culture of paganism! And at the same time, look what they did! They built their own churches on the old pagan sites where the pagan places of worship had been built! And why? Because, as the pagans well knew, that was where the earth's energy ley-lines were! And the invaders knew it too! Those early Christian invaders and desecrators certainly knew full well what they were doing!

Christianity is based on the Bible and on a male God who must be bowed down to and his instructions carried out. All the violence that has permeated history, all the torture and death, all the cruelty and persecution carried out in the name of Christianity would have been repudiated with nothing less than horror and revulsion by Jesus.

As would, indeed, the strongest image presented by the Christian Church, that iconic image of a crucified and dying Jesus on the cross! Is that what Jesus would have wanted? I sincerely doubt it!

The Church has indeed managed to bury and conceal a lot of truths about the life of Jesus.

Yes, Yeshua ben Joseph did exist, but he was not the Jesus of Nazareth depicted in the early church teachings.

But we can find the truth!   And we can find it in an unexpected place!

Where?

In the canonical gospels! It's there, hidden between the lines! In the tiniest detail!

If we take into consideration all the bias, and if we allow for all the re-editing, all the contradictions, all the historical inaccuracies, all the cover-ups, there is still vital information to be found in the residue. We do not need to throw out the baby with the bath water!

And we can see in many ways how the teachings of the church actually differ from the writings of the New Testament! Selective evidencing! Evidence for convenience!

The church has always presented us with a meek, mild and docile Jesus. But the gospels tell us differently! For example, when he cursed the fig tree for bearing no figs:

"The next day, as they were coming back from Bethany, Jesus was hungry. He saw in the distance a fig tree covered with leaves, so he went to see if he could find any figs on it. But when he came to it, he found only leaves, because it was not the right time for figs. Jesus said to the fig tree, 'No one shall ever eat figs from you again!' And his disciples heard him.............. Early next morning, as

they walked along the road, they saw the fig tree. It was dead all the way down to its roots. Peter remembered what had happened and said to Jesus, 'Look, Teacher, the fig tree you cursed has died!'
" (Mark 11:15-21)

"On his way back to the city early next evening, Jesus was hungry. He saw a fig tree by the side of the road and went to it, but found nothing on it except leaves. So he said to the tree, 'You will never again bear fruit!' At once the fig tree dried up." (Matthew 21:18-19)

And then there is the episode with the pigs, just after Jesus has performed an exorcism:

"There was a large herd of pigs near by, feeding on a hillside. So the spirits begged Jesus, 'Send us to the pigs, and let us go into them.' He let them go, and the evil spirits went off out of the man and entered the pigs. The whole herd, about 2,000 pigs in all, rushed down the side of the cliff and into the lake and was drowned." (Mark5:12-13)

And of course, how can we forget that Jesus wrecked the stalls in the Temple!

There is certainly nothing meek or mild about all of this! And as for docile! Docile is not even on the radar!

So why have the early church fathers presented Jesus as differently from the gospels?

Because they were not interested in the human Jesus! They were only interested in presenting a god-man who would be a model of obedience and subservience to the Roman authorities. For the same reasons as Paul taught in his letters about being obedient slaves and about paying your taxes. It was all Roman propaganda!

So what else can we find in the canonical gospels that church teachings have tried to bury and conceal?

Well, there is Mary Magdalene and the siblings of Jesus for a start! Not to mention Jesus' disciples and how they were all married and had their wives travelling with them, and how Peter had a mother-in-law!

And why all this cover-up?

To protect the Jesus of faith, the creation of Jesus the god-man and to protect the male-dominated church and its teaching of the virginity of Mary.

Yes, Jesus had brothers! But we have always been led to believe that he did not! Even though those same gospels on which the church has based its teachings tell us so!

In his first letter to the Corinthians, Paul writes: *"When people criticise me this is how I defend myself: 'Haven't I the right to follow the example of the other apostles and the Lord's brothers and Peter, by taking a Christian wife with me on my travels?"* (Corinthians I, 9:4-5)

And John mentions Jesus' brothers as well: *"Not even his brothers believed in him."* (John 7:5)

Even Josephus, the Jewish first-century historian tells us about Jesus' brother James: *"James, the brother of Jesus, the one they call messiah".*

Indeed, because of James' importance in the early Church, a letter attributed to him was included in the New Testament as the Epistle of James. But his leadership role put him in jeopardy during periods of persecution, and he was eventually put to death in

Jerusalem in 62 AD. And His death is recorded by the first-century Jewish historian Josephus, where he refers to James as '*the brother of Christ, the one they call the Messiah'*.

The gospels first mention James in Matthew 13:55: "*When Jesus finished telling these parables, he left that place and went back to his home town. He taught in the synagogue and those who heard him were amazed. 'Where did he get such wisdom?' they asked. 'And what about his miracles? Isn't he the carpenter's son? Isn't Mary his mother, and aren't James, Joseph, Simon and Judas his brothers? Aren't all his sisters living here?*" (Matthew 13:53-56)

And also in Mark 6:3, where he is listed along with three other brothers of Jesus and some un-named sisters. When Jesus went back to Nazareth and began teaching in the synagogue*: "Many people were there, and when they heard him they were all amazed. 'Where did he get all this?' they asked. 'What wisdom is this that has been given him? How does he perform miracles? Isn't this the carpenter, the son of Mary and the brother of James, Joseph, Judas and Simon? Aren't his sisters living here?*" (Mark: 6:2-3)

So according to a lot of people, Jesus had brothers!

Jesus had brothers? Yes, Jesus had brothers! So where did they come from?

The Catholic Church has always maintained that Jesus had no siblings! At other times, Church apologists have tried to explain that Joseph had children from a previous marriage, and therefore they were not the actual children of Mary.

The gospels clearly indicate otherwise! And we shall see why that is! In order to bolster the doctrine of the Perpetual Virginity of Mary!

As Jesus was the first-born of Mary, his brothers therefore, must have been younger than him!

"She gave birth to her first son......." (Luke 2:7)

"Jesus was still talking to the people when his mother and brothers arrived. They stood outside asking to speak with him. So some of the people there said to him, 'Look, your mother and brothers are standing outside, and they want to speak with you". (Matthew: 12:46-47)

And after the reported Resurrection, when Jesus appears to some of the disciples outside the tomb, he says: *"Go and tell my brothers to go to Galilee, and there they will see me".* (Matthew: 28:10)

Again, after the reported Ascension of Jesus, we read in Acts how:

"They gathered frequently to pray as a group, together with the women and with Mary the mother of Jesus and with his brothers". (Acts 1:14)

And we have also learned that he had sisters too! At least two of them!

Luke also talks about Jesus' brothers: *"Jesus' mother and brothers came to him, but were unable to join him because of the crowd".* (Luke 8:19)

And John: *"After this, Jesus and his mother, brothers and disciples went to Capernaum and stayed there a few days".* (John 2: 12)

And it was James, the brother of Jesus, who succeeded Jesus in his ministry. James, his brother, who succeeded him in the kingly line of David.

Not Peter! Peter whom we have been led to believe by the

Catholic Church was the first pope and successor of Jesus!

And why has the church insisted on establishing and perpetuating Peter as the successor to Jesus, and not his brother James? It's that perpetual virginity theory again! If Jesus is seen to have a brother, then that theory is dead in the water! So James has to be kept under wraps! Labelled *'Not for public consumption'*!

So where then, did all these siblings come from?

How do we find that out?

"That same day some Sadducees came to Jesus and claimed the people will not rise from death. 'Teacher', they said, 'Moses said that if a man who has no children dies, his brother must marry the widow so that they can have children who will be considered the dead man's children.' (Matthew 22: 23-24)

"If two brothers live on the same property and one of them dies, leaving no son, then his widow is not to be married to someone outside the family; it is the duty of the dead man's brother to marry her. The first son that they have will be considered the son of the dead man, so that his family line will continue in Israel. But if the dead man's brother does not want to marry her, she is to go before the town leaders and say, 'My husband's brother will not do his duty; he refuses to give his brother a descendant among the people of Israel.' Then the town leaders are to summon him and speak to him. If he still refuses to marry her, his brother's widow is to go up to him in the presence of the town leaders, take off one of his sandals, spit in his face, and say, 'This is what happens to the man who refuses to give his brother a descendant'. His family will be known in Israel as the family of the man who had his sandal pulled off". (Deuteronomy: 25:5-10)

So did Joseph's younger brother marry Mary after Joseph died? Tradition has it that Joseph was a lot older than Mary, so he probably died when Jesus was young, but why are we not told about this? Obviously, again, to divert us from the truth that Mary remarried, and had further children! That would mean exit '*blessed Mary ever virgin*'! End of! Nicene Creed good bye!

Further evidence for the importance of James' role is found in the Gospel of Thomas. The Gospel of Thomas was one of the Gospels found in Egypt, hidden in the desert, near Nag Hammadi in 1945. According to Saying 12 of this Gospel, the disciples said to Jesus:

" 'We are aware that you will depart from us. Who will be our leader?'

Jesus answered: 'No matter where you come from, it is to James the Just that you shall go, for whose sake heaven and earth have come to exist.' "

This passage clearly indicates that Jesus designated James to take over the leadership of his ministry after his death. I wonder why this Gospel of Thomas did not find its way into the canonical gospels?

Some Christians think that James was actually a step-brother of Jesus, or possibly only a cousin, because they believe that Mary remained a virgin throughout her life and therefore couldn't have given birth to any children except Jesus. But Matthew, Mark, Paul, together with the early historians Josephus and Hegesippus all appear to say that James was a full brother, and most modern scholars have reached the same conclusion.

And what about Mary Magdalene? Why has the church kept her under wraps for 2,000 years? Why has she been buried by the early Christian church?

We just have to face the fact that there is no such thing as the 'Gospel truth', and Mary Magdalene is another one of the victims.

Mary Magdalene is synonymous with the long-oppressed feminine side of the story of Christianity, the defeminisation of the early Christian Church, Mary Magdalene, who she was and the life she played in the part of Jesus is the subject of my next book 'Behind Every Great Man... Mary Magdalene Twin Flame of Jesus'.

So we can see the lengths to which the early Christian church fathers went in order to bury the real Jesus, the human Yeshua. And not just to bury him, but to bury his family and Mary Magdalene as well! Those early Christian Church fathers were not in the least interested in presenting Yeshua the man. They wanted and needed some sort of super-man. Some sort of idol whom people would worship! A god! Straight out of heaven! An 'only begotten son of God'! A god who would give the other Roman gods and goddesses a run for their money!

Let us now look at some of the later dogmas and doctrines of the church which were brought in to make sure that the real Jesus was well and truly buried, and would never be found again!

CHAPTER 4

Church dogmas, doctrines and teachings

Jesus and his teachings have been swallowed up, buried under church dogma after dogma after dogma, the whole basic point of his teachings being completely misrepresented to us. It is now time for us to consider some of these main dogmas, doctrines and teachings of the Roman Catholic Church that have been presented to us down through the centuries. Those doctrines and dogmas that have been perpetrated and cemented in concrete to instil fear and guilt into us in order to keep us submissive, subservient, docile, obedient! Those doctrines and dogmas that were necessary to have Jesus to be seen to compete with the other gods of the time such as Osiris, Adonis, Mithras, all born of virgins and all raised from the dead.

The Council of Nicaea, 325 C.E., convened by the Roman Emperor Constantine to bring some sort of order and cohesion to the teachings of the new fledgling church, produced the Nicene Creed, which is still recited today by millions of church goers throughout the world and believed by them to contain the irrefutable truths about God and Jesus.

So let us take a look at this Nicene Creed:

'I believe in one God / the Father, the Almighty, / creator of heaven and earth, / of all that is seen and unseen. / I believe in one Lord, Jesus Christ, / the only Son of God, / eternally begotten of the Father. / Through him all things were made. / For us men and for our salvation / he came down from heaven: / by the power of the Holy Spirit / he became incarnate of the Virgin Mary, and was

made man. / For our sake he was crucified under Pontius Pilate; /
he suffered death and was buried. / On the third day he rose again
/ in accordance with the Scriptures; / he ascended into heaven /
and is seated at the right hand of the Father. / He will come again
in glory to judge the living and the dead, / and his kingdom will
have no end. / We believe in the Holy Spirit, the Lord, the giver of
Life, / who proceeds from the Father and the Son. / Together with
the Father and the Son he is worshipped and glorified. / He has
spoken through the Prophets. / We believe in one holy catholic and
apostolic Church. / We acknowledge one baptism for the
forgiveness of sins./ We look for the resurrection of the dead, / and
the life of the world to come. Amen.

This was the main dogma and doctrine that came out of the
Council at Nicaea, 325 C.E! That Council of Nicaea, convened by
the Emperor Constantine to bring some sort of order and cohesion
into the newly-fledged Christian Church!

But how much of this Nicene Creed is based on the teachings of
Jesus? Very little, if any of it! And how much of this Nicene Creed is
based on the later teachings of Paul, who disagreed with Jesus'
immediate successors over Jesus' teachings, and on later
innovations of the early Christian church fathers? Almost all of it!

The death of Jesus on the cross and his subsequent resurrection
are pivotal to the beliefs of Christianity. Apart from the doctrines
and dogmas on the Death and Resurrection of Jesus, other main
doctrines and dogmas include the Doctrine of the Divinity of Jesus;
the Doctrine of the Immaculate Conception; the Doctrine of the
Perpetual Virginity of Mary; the Doctrine of the Assumption of
Mary; the Doctrine of the Eucharist, and the Doctrine of Papal
Infallibility. These all form the basis on which the teachings of the
Roman Catholic Church are founded.

So where did all these church dogmas and doctrines originate?

The latter, the Doctrine of Papal Infallibility was declared and dogmatically defined by the First Vatican Council, 1869, under the auspices of Pope Pius IX, Pope from 1846-1878. A very clever move, obviously, to keep all in subservience to church teachings! It reminds one of the final stage, right down through history, when each and every time a dictator managed to take complete and total power into his own hands!

So that doctrine certainly did not originate with Jesus! And it is not to be found in any gospels!

The *'Doctrine of the Perpetual Virginity of Mary'* declares that Mary was a virgin, not just when Jesus was born, but throughout the rest of her life as well. This idea was first mentioned by the Christian theologian Epiphanus in 374 C.E. and was affirmed by both the Second Council of Constantinople in 553 C.E. and the Lateran Council in 649 C.E. This Second Council of Constantinople had gone ahead despite being forbidden by the then pope, Vigilius, who did not attend.

This teaching of the *'Perpetual Virginity'* is simply not found in the New Testament nor is it found in any of the earliest Christian creeds. Although it is a firmly established part of Catholic teaching, the truth is that it has never actually been declared an infallible dogma by the Roman Catholic Church. Most of the early Christian writers before the late fourth century C.E. simply took for granted that the brothers and sisters of Jesus were the natural-born offspring of Mary and Joseph.

The Roman Catholic Church has always insisted that Jesus did not actually have any siblings. This theory is, of course, meant to support and upholster the theory of the Perpetual Virginity of

Mary. Even where the gospels say that Jesus had brothers, the Church teachings insist that they are not related to Jesus by blood because they were not the children of his mother, Mary. Very much a case of the Church selecting what suits and discarding what does not suit!

Of the four canonical gospels, only two mention the birth of Jesus, that of Matthew and that of Luke. A virgin birth is certainly not an ordinary occurrence, by any stretch of the imagination! And yet two out of the four authors of the gospels do not even mention it!

And if Mary was indeed a virgin before the conception of Jesus, then she certainly did not retain her virginity after she had given birth to all the siblings of Jesus! The Church even tried to explain all this by declaring that the term 'brothers' was a generic term, not specifically referring to those born of the same mother, but more in the way of 'cousins', in just the same way perhaps as Shakespeare uses the generic greeting 'cousin' as a form of recognition or greeting. It was even claimed that Jesus' brothers were the sons of Joseph by a previous marriage. But this is not what we learn in the gospels or the writings of the New Testament. Selective evidencing indeed! History according to convenience! Word-play for manipulation! Spin!

The 'Doctrine of the Assumption of Mary' declares that Mary was taken up into Heaven, since she had no sinful nature, not having been involved in any sinful activities, including sex. This doctrine was first declared and defined as an article of faith by Pope Pius XIII in 1950.

But where in the Bible does it tell us about this?

The newly converted Roman Emperor Constantine had convoked the first ecumenical council of the Christian Church at Nicaea in

325. The opinions of the attending bishops were anything but unanimous, and it was the young Athanasius, later Bishop of Alexandria, whose word held sway. Under Athanasius' direction, the Council of Nicaea determined that Christ was *"begotten, not made"*, and was *"of the same substance as the Father"*.

At the First Council of Constantinople in 381, under the emperor Theodosius I, the doctrine of the *'Three Persons in One, the Father, Son and Holy Spirit'* declared that all three, while being distinct from one another, were still equal in their eternity and power. Now it was possible to teach, as Nicaea had, that Christ was *"of the same substance as the Father"*.

The relations between the Divine and the human aspects in the one person, Jesus Christ, continued to be a matter of strong debate at the Council of Ephesus in 431, until it was finally settled at the Council of Chalcedon in 451. This doctrine became known as the *'Doctrine of the Divinity of Jesus'*. The basis for the settlement was adopted from the declaration of Pope Leo I, pope from 440 until 461:

"We all unanimously teach.....one and the same Son, Our Lord Jesus Christ, perfect in deity and perfect in humanity....in two natures, without being mixed, transmuted, divided, or separated. The distinction between the natures is by no means done away with through the union, but rather the identity of each nature is preserved and concurs into one person and being."

This has been the basic statement of the doctrine of the person of Christ for most of the Church ever since. Leo I, also known as Saint Leo the Great, was noted for his meeting with Attila the Hun in 452 and persuading him to abandon his invasion of Italy.

So the *'Doctrine of the Divinity of Jesus'*, that holds that Jesus was

Eileen McCourt

of Divine nature, that he was the Son of God, God in human form, dates from the Council of Chalcedon in 451 C.E.

It is these doctrines, - the doctrine of the Immaculate Conception, the doctrine of the Perpetual Virginity of Mary, the doctrine of the Assumption of Mary, the doctrine of the Divinity of Jesus, together with the doctrines of the Eucharist, the Crucifixion, the Death and Resurrection of Jesus, and the doctrine of Papal Infallibility, form the basis on which the teachings of the Roman Catholic Church are founded.

But these doctrines did not come from Jesus! They came from early church men!

Dogmas, dogmas and more dogmas! All from early and succeeding church men!

But not even one of these doctrines is rooted in historical evidence, or indeed in scripture! These are theological views driven solely by theological concerns that have nothing at all to do with the earliest traditions about Jesus and his family!

These doctrines do not come from the teachings of Jesus! They are a mixture of the ancient Roman and Greek pagan beliefs in their venerated deities of myth and legend trundling down through history, resurrected once again for mercenary purposes and to prop up a patriarchal institution for whom lust for power and control was paramount over all other concerns.

These doctrines are sourced in mythology! These doctrines have written Jesus out of Christianity rather than into Christianity!

The Church has, for 2,000 years, fostered and paraded in front of us the image of a judgemental, punishing God, sitting up on his high throne in Heaven, bolstered up by his sole offspring, his male,

52

celibate son called Jesus, and the virgin mother of Jesus, called Mary!

As well as the Nicene Creed, the Council at Nicaea promulgated twenty new church laws called canons, unchanging rules of discipline. All to do with structuring the new hierarchical, patriarchal, male-dominated Christian Church! The Church that the early church fathers proclaimed as being based on the teachings of Jesus!

Jesus did not see himself as God or of a divine nature any more than everyone else is of divine nature. That was what people then did not understand. The divinity of ALL men! And yes! The early Christian Church fathers went to great lengths to expound the Divinity of Jesus. What they failed to acknowledge was the Divinity of Man!

Jesus did not come to found a new religion or a new church, any more than Martin Luther intended to do so! Like Martin Luther, Jesus simply wanted to reform what was already there. The Spiritual enlightenment of men has not been attempted to any degree, and the requirements of the Church have always been that we should strictly obey the dogmas and tenets declared by the priests and ecclesiastical hierarchy.

But observing the dogmas, creeds and teachings of the Church is NOT going to get any of us anywhere in the spirit world! Observing the dogmas, creeds and teachings of the Church is NOT going to get any of us onto a higher energy vibrational level! And raising ourselves up to a higher Spiritual energy vibration level is exactly and precisely what we all need to do!

And neither Jesus nor even God can do that for us! And the Christian Church certainly cannot do it! No matter how well we obey all their laws! Only we ourselves can do it! Each one for himself!

The Christian Church is all outwards advocating, not inwards! And why? Because if its members turn inwards, then the church has no longer got control over them!

The world of flamboyant ceremonial vestments, elaborate ceremonies, was NOT the world of Jesus!

The world of an angry, punishing God was NOT the world of Jesus!

The world of a patriarchal society, with rigid hierarchal structures was NOT the world of Jesus!

The world of paying lip service, rhymed off patterns of prayer was NOT the world of Jesus!

The world of rigid, unbending dogmas was NOT the world of Jesus!

The world of fear and control through fear was NOT the world of Jesus!

So, in order to find the real Jesus, the Yeshua of first-century Palestine, we have to look beyond church teachings and dogmas, because we will most certainly NOT find him there!

There will be no resurrection of bodies on the last day! There will not even be a last day! That is all false teaching! And no-one is going to spend eternity in any sort of hell. We are ALL destined for perfection!

And who created all the saints? Who decided all that? No church authority here on earth has the power to elevate souls in the spirit world, or to affect in any way what happens there! That is spiritual arrogance on the part of the Church hierarchies! Each soul is responsible for its own evolution. There is not, and cannot be, any church giving of a leg-up towards sainthood! No church on earth can decide at what level any soul is at in the Spiritual hierarchy!

We can no longer exonerate ourselves or hide behind the dogmas, doctrines and teachings of the church. We must take responsibility for our own soul evolution, instead of sauntering through life believing that if we obey the rules of the church, then that church will guarantee us a place in heaven.

"O wretched mortals, open your eyes!"

CHAPTER 5

The Many Interpretations of Jesus

There is no such thing as alternative facts! Despite what President Trump has said! Yes, there are multiple alternative interpretations and multiple alternative opinions. But there is no such thing as alternative facts!

No other figure in history has influenced humanity to anything like the degree Jesus has. He is everywhere! In all genres of Literature; in music; in song and dance; in films; in sculpture; in all forms of art. You just cannot fail to spot him!

The New Testament itself records only a fragment of what Jesus taught. And what was written down was tampered with by numerous editors, or suppressed.

So who exactly was Jesus? That is what this book attempts to explain! As always, the answer is steeped in controversy.

On the one hand, we have the classic conservative orthodox Western Christian belief about Jesus, the Jesus who is accepted and believed in by millions around the world. Here we have the deified, super-human Jesus, the Messiah, born of a virgin, the supernatural son of a supernatural God, that same God who sent his only son down to earth to die on the cross to atone for the sins of all mankind, earning us forgiveness, redemption and eternal life through his suffering and death. This same Jesus was endowed with supernatural powers, proving his divine nature and identity. He healed the sick, he raised people from the dead. Then he himself was raised from the dead, after which he ascended into heaven, where he now sits beside the throne of God, from where he continues to watch over us, monitoring us, and pleading with his father on our behalf. Before he left us he established his church, the Christian Church, giving power to Peter and his successors to forgive us our sins.

On the other hand, we have the more modern idea about Jesus, the Jesus who has come to be seen as an ordinary man, a teacher, a healer. This Jesus probably did not perform all those miracles attributed to him in the canonical gospels. Were they not all Roman propaganda, stories built up around the prophecies in the Old Testament, stories intended to deify this Jesus and show he was indeed the son of God? Is it not true that those who wrote these stories about the life of Jesus were not his immediate disciples? Is it not true that these gospels were written forty years and more after the death of Jesus? Were these stories not handed down orally through all those years? Is it not true that Jesus himself never intended to found a new church? That he never saw himself as a supernatural son of God? That he certainly never rose from the dead or ascended bodily into heaven? Is it not true that Jesus himself was not a Christian, the word itself not yet having been coined?

There is one thing we can say for sure! Both of these juxtaposed views cannot be true! Either Jesus was born of a virgin or he was not. Either he performed all those miracles or he did not. Either he died on the cross for our sins or he did not. Either he rose from the dead or he did not. Either he ascended into heaven or he did not.

Then there are those who claim that Jesus never existed. A myth, created by the early Christian church in order to compete with all the other religions that had their gods and goddesses.

So what are we supposed to believe?

Let's take a look at some of the interpretations about Jesus that have been aired recently. And yes, some do make for sensational reading! But let each reader decide for himself!

First of all, do we know what Jesus looked like? Yes, we do have some descriptions. One letter which is believed to have been sent to the Roman Senate by Publius Lentulus, governor of Judea before Pontius Pilate, describes Jesus as possessing a "*singular beauty, surpassing the children of men*", and an "*excellent body proportion*".

And in a further letter from Publius Lentulus to Tiberius Caesar, Roman Emperor:

'A man of noble stature and of very beautiful countenance, in which such majesty resides that those who look on him are forced to admire him. His hair is of the color of a fully ripe chestnut, and from his ear down his shoulders it is of the color of the earth, but shining. It is parted in the middle of his forehead, after the manner of the Nazarenes.

His forehead is smooth and very serene, his face free from wrinkle and spot, and with a slight color.......the beard is thick, and, like the hair, not very long, and divided in the middle..........there is a look of terror in his grave eyes. The eyes are like the rays of the sun, and it is impossible to look him steadily in the face on account of their brilliance...........when he reproves, he terrifies; when he admonishes, he weeps. He makes himself loved, and is gravely cheerful. It is said that he was never seen to laugh, but he was seen to weep.........in learning he is an object of wonder to the entire city of Jerusalem. He never studied at all, and yet he knows all sciences........he wears sandals, and goes bareheaded. Many laugh at seeing him; but in his presence, and when speaking to him, they fear and tremble..........It is said that such a man was never seen or heard in these parts. In truth, as the Hebrews tell me, there never were heard such advices, such sublime doctrine as this Christ teaches; and many of the Jews hold him for divine, and they believe in him, while many others accuse him to me as being contrary to thy majesty.......it is acknowledged that he has never done harm to any one, but good. All that know him and have had dealings with him, say that they have received from him benefits and health.'

However, reports differ greatly, for example, Jesus' hair is sometimes described as golden, sometimes as reddish, other times as reddish-brown and most scholars dismiss all this as medieval fabrications. Jesus is even described as fair-skinned with blue eyes. But surely, as a first-century Jew born in the Middle East, Jesus would have had swarthy skin, dark hair and dark eyes?

We also have a letter from Pontius Pilate to the Roman Emperor Tiberius Caesar, concerning Jesus, copies of which are in the Congressional Library in Washington D.C. Pontius Pilate was the Roman official who gave the final order for the crucifixion of Jesus. According to the canonical gospels, he actually believed that Jesus was innocent and could find no fault with him. He wanted to save him, but was pressured into condemning him by the disorderly mob and the Jewish religious authorities who saw Jesus as a troublesome radical, endangering their power and authority. Pilate was the fifth prefect of the Roman province of Judea from 26-36 C.E., serving under Emperor Tiberius Caesar.

Pilate wrote, describing the physical appearance of Jesus:

"A young man appeared in Galilee preaching with humble unction, a new man in the Name of God that had sent Him. At first I was

59

apprehensive that His design was to stir up trouble against the Romans, but my fears were dispelled. Jesus of Nazareth spoke rather as a friend of the Romans than of the Jews. One day I observed in the midst of a group of people a young man who was leaning against a tree, calmly addressing the multitude. I was told it was Jesus. This I could easily have suspected so great was the difference between Him and those who were listening to Him. His golden colored hair and beard gave to his appearance a celestial aspect. He appeared to be about 30 years of age. Never have I seen a sweeter or more serene countenance. What a contrast between Him and His bearers with their black beards and tawny complexions......................

Later, I wrote to Jesus requesting an interview with Him at the Praetorium. He came. When the Nazarene made his appearance I was having my morning walk and as I faced Him my feet seemed fastened with an iron hand to the marble pavement and I trembled in every limb as a guilty culprit, though he was calm. For some time I stood admiring this extraordinary Man. There was nothing in Him that was repelling, nor in his character, yet I felt awed in His presence. I told Him that there was a magnetic simplicity about Him and His personality that elevated Him far above the philosophers and teachers of His day.

Now, Noble Sovereign, these are the facts concerning Jesus of Nazareth and I have taken the time to write you in detail concerning these matters. I say that such a man who could convert water to wine, change death into life, disease into health; calm the stormy sea, is not guilty of any criminal offense and as others have said, we must agree---truly this is the Son of God.

Your most obedient servant, Pontius Pilate" (Taken from the New Advent; Fathers of the Church)

Secondly, why did Jesus hang around with those who were considered to be the undesirables of society of his day, prostitutes and tax collectors?

"A large number of tax collectors and other outcasts were following Jesus, and many of them joined him and his disciples at the table." (Mark 2:15)

Jesus was accused of being *"a glutton and a drunkard and a friend of tax collectors and other outcasts".* (Matthew 11:19) (Luke 7:34)

"When John (Baptist) came, he fasted and drank no wine, and everyone said, 'He has a demon in him!' When the Son of Man came, he ate and drank, and everyone said, 'Look at this man! He is a glutton and a drinker, a friend of tax collectors and other outcasts!' " (Matthew 11:18-19)

Certainly the gospels portray Jesus as someone who enjoyed sharing meals, in contrast to John the Baptist who was known for his frugal life-style and restraint in both eating and drinking. On the other hand, the gospels do not give us any information about Jesus ever behaving drunkenly, disorderly or inappropriately. In fact we have many examples of Jesus abstaining from food and drink, for example during the forty days in the desert.

And as for the company he kept, well, were these not the very people Jesus wanted to help? Were these not the very people who needed him the most?

"Some teachers of the Law, who were Pharisees, saw that Jesus was eating with these outcasts and tax collectors, so they asked his disciples, 'Why does he eat with such people?' Jesus heard them and answered, 'People who are well do not need a doctor, but only

those who are sick. I have not come to call respectable people, but outcasts." (Mark 2:16-17)

Thirdly, was Jesus suicidal? On a self-destruct mission? Castigating the powerful Jewish authorities,- the Pharisees, the Sadducees and the High Priests of the Temple, deliberately confronting them and antagonising them in front of the crowds? Jesus did not conform to their ideas or to societal expectations. He was constantly provocative and showed little concern for his own reputation, persistently subverting first-century Jewish conventions and customs. Although he lived in a patriarchal and homophobic society, Jesus showed he did not share their prejudices.

For example, in John's Gospel (John 4:7-27) we read about how he spoke to the Samaritan woman at the well, the Samaritans being considered to be the lowliest section of society, and even his own disciples reprimanded him for engaging in any sort of conversation with her.

Then on another occasion (John 8:5-7) he prevented the application of the Jewish Law of stoning to a woman who had committed adultery.

And on numerous occasions he disregarded the Jewish rules about the Sabbath, and of course again ended up, yet again, in confrontations over the same with the Pharisees and Sadducees.

In my previous book, *'Are Ye Not Gods?'* I posed the question that if you could ask Jesus one question, just one, then what would that one question be?

The Pharisees asked him: *'Who do you think you are?'* (John 8:53)

And what would my one question be? I would have to ask Jesus what did he think he was doing? And I now have my answer! Jesus knew perfectly well what he was doing! He was on a mission to get himself crucified! To get himself crucified in order to fulfil the gospels! I will explain all this in later chapters!

He was even rude to those who invited him to dine with them!

In Luke 7:36-50, Jesus is invited to the house of a Pharisee, and a woman, known as a local prostitute comes in, cries tears over Jesus' feet, wipes them with her hair, and then pours perfume on them. Contrary to expectations, Jesus reprimands the Pharisee, not the woman:

" *'Do you see this woman? I came into your home, and you gave me no water for mu feet, but she has washed my feet with her tears, and dried them with her hair. You did not welcome me with a kiss, but she has not stopped kissing my feet since I came. You provided me with no olive oil for my head, but she has covered my feet with perfume.'* " (Luke 7:44-46)

Jesus did not see a prostitute in front of him. He saw a spiritual light, the spiritual light we all carry within ourselves.

Was Jesus mad, or even a raving lunatic? Some people around him seemed to have thought so!

"Then Jesus went home. Again such a large crowd gathered that Jesus and his disciples had no time to eat. When his family heard about it, they set out to take charge of him, because people were saying, 'He's gone mad!' " (Mark 3:20-21)

Was he possessed by the devil? Some thought so!

"Some teachers of the Law who had come from Jerusalem were saying, 'He has Beelzebub in him! It is the chief of the demons who gives him the power to drive them out.' " (Mark3:22)

"They asked Jesus, '*Were we not right in saying that you are a Samaritan and have a demon in you?*' " (John 8:48)

Was he a superstar? He certainly had crowds following him!

The Church has always presented us with a meek, mild and docile Jesus. But the gospels tell us differently! For example, as we saw earlier, when he cursed the fig tree for bearing no figs. Could he not have blessed it instead and sent some good energy to it, enabling it to produce fruit?

And then, as we also saw earlier, there is the episode with the pigs, just after Jesus has performed an exorcism:

"There was a large herd of pigs nearby, feeding on a hillside. So the spirits begged Jesus, 'Send us to the pigs, and let us go into them.' He let them go, and the evil spirits went off out of the man and entered the pigs. The whole herd, about 2,000 pigs in all, rushed down the side of the cliff and into the lake and was drowned." (Mark 5:12-13)

Those pigs were someone's livestock, someone's livelihood! And Jesus destroyed them!

And of course, how can we forget that Jesus wrecked the stalls in the Temple!

And he could reprove!

"Then Jesus called the crowd to him once more and said to them, 'Listen to me, all of you, and understand. There is nothing that goes into a person from the outside which can make him unclean. Rather, it is what comes out of a person that makes him unclean.'

*When he left the crowd and went into the house, his disciples asked him to explain this saying. '**You are no more intelligent than the others', Jesus said to them. 'Don't you understand?'** '* (Mark 7:14-18)

That wasn't very complimentary!

Was Jesus gay? Did he and his beloved disciple, '*the disciple whom Jesus loved*' share a homosexual relationship? Homosexuality and bisexuality were certainly not uncommon in Jesus' time, and did not carry the stigma of more recent times. Furthermore, young men or older boys were frequently initiated into the sexual act by older men. We read in Mark's gospel, how, when Jesus was being arrested in the Garden of Gethsemane:

"A certain young man, dressed only in a linen cloth, was following Jesus. They tried to arrest him, but he ran away naked, leaving the cloth behind." (Mark 14:51)

So, what was going on there, one could well ask! Remember, this was first-century Jewish Palestine, not twenty-first century anywhere! We need to think in first-century terms in order to empathise! There is a balance of male and female in each and every one of us, reflecting the balance of Father-Mother God in the entirety of Creation. We have all had past lives as both male and female, in order to find that balance within ourselves. The reason why this is such a warring, hostile, aggressive world right now is because there is a dominance of the masculine, an imbalance of the masculine-feminine. We see tolerance and understanding in Jesus' words:

" 'For there are different reasons why men cannot marry: some because they were born that way; others, because men made them that way; and others do not marry for the sake of the Kingdom of heaven. Let him who can accept this teaching do so.' " (Matthew 19: 12)

Was Jesus married? He is constantly referred to in the canonical gospels as *'Teacher'* or *'Rabbi'*. A Jewish Rabbi was expected to be married.

Was Jesus a women's liberator? Certainly, he had women travelling with him, and supporting him:

"Some time later Jesus travelled through towns and villages,

preaching the Good News about the Kingdom of God. The twelve disciples went with him, and so did some women who had been healed of evil spirits and diseases: Mary (who was called Magdalene) from whom seven demons had been driven out; Joanna, whose husband Chuza was an officer in Herod's court; and Susanna, and many other women who used their own resources to help Jesus and his disciples." (Luke 8:1-34)

And then what do we make from the fact that one of these women was Joanne, "whose *husband Chuza was an officer in Herod's court."?*

Was Jesus a fraud? Trying to establish himself and his family as the rightful rulers of Israel?

Was he an itinerant cult leader?

A devious schemer?

A sorcerer? A magician?

A man with a political agenda?

A shaman-prophet?

A man simply attempting to fulfil the prophecies?

A man determined to make his life mirror the ancient Gods, the myths of antiquity?

A man interchangeable with other deities and other Gods?

Was Jesus a violent revolutionary? He was certainly surrounded by Zealots and people who carried knives! Remember how the ear of the centurion was cut off? And by none other than Peter!

" 'But now,' Jesus said, 'whoever has a purse or a bag must take it,

and whoever has no sword must sell his coat and buy one.' " (Luke 22:36)

Was Jesus illegitimate? In the New International Version of the Bible we read:

"They answered Jesus, 'We are not illegitimate children,' they protested, 'The only Father we have is God himself. ' "

And in the New Living Translation:

"No, you are imitating your real father.' They replied. 'We aren't illegitimate children! God himself is our true Father."

And again, in the English Standard Translation:

" 'You are doing the works your father did.' They said to him, 'We were not born of sexual immorality. We have one Father - even God.' "

Was this all a personal dig at Jesus, suggesting that he was illegitimate?

We have always been led to believe that the least we can expect of Jesus is that he was good!

"As Jesus was starting on his way again, a man ran up, knelt before him, and asked him, 'Good Teacher, what must I do to receive eternal life?'

'Why do you call me good?' Jesus asked him. 'No one is good except God alone.' " (Mark 10:18)

Indeed, contradictions certainly abound!

"Jesus knew that they were about to come and seize him in order to make him king by force, se he went off again to the hills by

himself." (John 6:15)

Yet at other times they were trying to kill him!

Jesus clearly spelt out that a rich man cannot enter the Kingdom of God. Yet Joseph of Arimathea, his own uncle, referred to in the gospels as 'a rich man', was the one who took Jesus down from the cross and buried him in his own tomb. Joseph of Arimathea was one of the wealthiest men in Judea, a tin miner, with a vast fleet of ships travelling across the Mediterranean to the tin mines of southern Britain, carrying back tin for the Roman armies. He was also a member of the prestigious Jewish Sanhedrin, the powerful ruling elite force who controlled all aspects of Jewish lives. And he was Jesus' uncle, the brother of Jesus' mother, Mary!

Jesus often told people they had to give up everything in order to follow him. He instructed the rich young man:

" *'Go, sell what you own, and give the money to the poor, and you will have treasure in heaven; the come, follow me.' "* (Mark 10:21)

Yet his disciples themselves did not give up everything! Even though Peter reminded Jesus: "*Look, we have left everything and followed you*", clearly they had not! For example, Simon Peter and Andrew retained their home in Capernaum:

"Jesus and his disciples, including James and John, left the synagogue and went straight to the home of Simon and Andrew". (Mark 1:29)

And Levi/ Matthew gave Jesus a dinner party with friends at his home: *"Later on Jesus was having a meal in Levi's house....."* (Mark 2:15)

And indeed, we are often told that Jesus "*went home*".

Peter retained his fishing boat, nets and gear, as related in John 21:3 at the miracle of the fishes. Mary and Martha repeatedly opened their home to Jesus and his disciples, and the women supported Jesus with their financial means:

"...........And many other women who used their own resources to help Jesus and his disciples." (Luke 8:2-3)

Again, a paradox in Jesus' teaching! On the one hand, wealth seems necessary for survival, and indeed can enable one to do good, and yet at the same time it can be a barrier to following and serving Jesus wholeheartedly, *" No one can be a slave of two masters.... You cannot serve both God and money".* (Matthew 6:24)

So how can we unravel the enigma that was Jesus?

The only answer?

We cannot!

All we can say is that he is as he is!

PART THREE: JESUS LOST AND FOUND

CHAPTER 6

The setting: First-century Jewish Palestine

The greatest story ever told!

Or, indeed the greatest story never told!

We need to set the scene. We need some stage scenery! We need to establish the back-drop!

We need to consider what it would have been like to be born into this time, the early first century C.E., and into this place, Judaic Judea.

Certainly we all have a lot of visual images in our mind. Images created by such as Shakespeare's 'Anthony and Cleopatra' or 'Julius Caesar', for example, or George Bernard Shaw's 'Androcles and the Lion', the epic films 'Ben Hur' or 'Quo Vadis', the musicals 'Jesus Christ, Super-Star', or 'Godspell' or even the more modern novel 'The Da Vinci Code'. All written or created, not as historical documents, not as historical evidence, but as forms of entertainment, with the purpose of scoring box-office hits. Very often however, the idea is given to us first in books and films, making us think, opening us up to the potentiality of the truth. Then it is accepted!

So what was life really like in first-century Jewish Palestine? What more can we find out about this ancient land of Judea, home to the Jewish religion Judaism? The story that has been presented to us all these years, the story of the birth of a child called Jesus in

Bethlehem at the time of Herod; his growing up in Nazareth; his teaching in the temple; his betrayal by Judas; his crucifixion and death on the cross for our sins, to redeem mankind; his raising again from the dead and his ascension into heaven?

Let us delve deeper! Let us delve further into the historical facts!

Judea in the time of Jesus was not a peaceful country. It was a political and religious furnace, a hot-bed, a smouldering, simmering, churning ethnic cauldron of dissent and hatred, with constant eruptions. This world into which Yeshua was born was torn apart by the religious and political power of the Pharisees and the Sadducees on the one hand, and by the political and military power of the Romans on the other. It was awash with bandits and insurgent groups, messianic prophets declaring that the time of God's intervention to save his people the Israelites, was at hand. Apocalyptic expectation among the Jews was high, with numerous prophets, preachers and self-designated messiahs delivering the message of the imminent judgement and the imminent coming of God to rescue his people, the Israelites, from the hated rule of the oppressive Romans. Hopeful messiahs wandered the land, preaching and warning of the impending end of time, the final clash, the final show-down between the forces of good and the forces of evil.

We must keep in mind that all such movements in first-century Jewish Palestine were both religious and political, not simply one or the other. Roman oppression was going to be ended by the imminent coming of the messiah, the messiah who would end Roman oppression by restoring God's kingdom on earth. Politics and religious beliefs were inter-mingled, inter-connected, inseparable. Hence it is that we cannot consider Jesus simply in religious terms, but also in political terms. Yes, Jesus like all the other religious teachers of his day, was also a political figure! And like all the others, caught up in political intrigue!

In fact, Jesus was a very political figure! He directly challenged and rebuked the religious and political authorities of his day. And who were these authorities?

The Pharisees and the Sadducees, not to mention the priests of the Temple! But these were not just religious leaders. These were also the political leaders of Israel during Jesus' time. Judea had been conquered by the Romans and was now occupied territory. But the Romans handed over authority to their local puppets, and did not interfere in the internal ruling of the country as long as the money from taxes continued to pour into the Roman coffers. In Judea, the local leaders were the Sanhedrin, dominated by the Sadducees, and ruled by the High Priest. In return for being puppets, the Sadducees kept their wealth and privileged positions secure.

Yeshua continually rebuked the Pharisees and Sadducees for their hypocrisy, their wide-scale corruption and their misinterpretations and manipulation of the Law:

'How terrible for you, teachers of the Law and Pharisees! You hypocrites! You clean the outside of your cup and plate, while the inside is full of what you have obtained by violence and selfishness. Blind Pharisees!

How terrible for you, teachers of the Law and Pharisees! You hypocrites! You are like whitewashed tombs, which look fine on the outside but are full of bones and decaying corpses on the inside, In the same way, on the outside you appear good to everybody, but inside you are full of hypocrisy and sins.' (Matthew 23:25-28)

The Pharisees and Sadducees in turn retaliated, constantly testing

Jesus by asking him to show a sign from heaven:

'Some Pharisees and Sadducees who came to Jesus wanted to trap him, so they asked him to perform a miracle for them, to show that God approved of him.' (Matthew 16:1)

'Then the Pharisees left and made plans to kill Jesus.' (Matthew 12:14)

'The Pharisees went off and made a plan to trap Jesus with questions.' (Matthew 22:15)

'Even then, many of the Jewish authorities believed in Jesus; but because of the Pharisees they did not talk about it openly so as not to to be expelled from the synagogue. They loved human approval rather than the approval of God.' (John 12:42-43)

In Judea, the Jewish leaders were particularly powerful because Pontius Pilate, the Roman Governor of Judea, was particularly weak, and was easily humiliated by them. And it was these powerful forces that Jesus constantly challenged!

He challenged not just their political power structure, but also the financial source of their power, and their corrupt methods. Corruption was endemic in politics and government. Nothing new there then! All sounds familiar!

The Jewish High Priest Annas was a sort of mafia leader, using his wealth to bribe the Roman governors to appoint his cronies, mostly family members, to various important positions in the government of Judea. He had already secured his own appointment as high priest of Judea, the most powerful Jewish position in the land, and now he got five of his sons and one son-in-law appointed to the same position. Religion and politics were combined as the high priest of Judea was also the chairman of the powerful Sanhedrin.

And how these powerful men obtained their wealth was also a matter of concern to Jesus. And here religion and politics were most definitely inter-twined!

The high priest controlled the goings on in the Temple, profiting from the vast amount of money that exchanged hands in the selling of sacrificial animals and the exchange of money that constantly went on in the Temple courtyards on a daily basis.

Only the bravest of souls would have dared to challenge these powerful authorities and question their methods of using religion and the Torah to prey on the poor.

And Jesus' clearing of the Temple was certainly, in their eyes, going too far!

Jesus even challenged them about how they treated the poor:

'You hypocrites! You give a tenth even of the seasoning herbs, such as mint, dill and cumin, but you neglect to obey the really important teachings of the law, such as justice and mercy and honesty. These you should practise, without neglecting the others.' (Matthew 23:23-24)

So we can see that religion and politics were not separable in Jesus' time. In fact, Jesus himself said, at the beginning of his public ministry:

'The Spirit of the Lord is upon me, because he has chosen me to bring good news to the poor. He has sent me to proclaim liberty to the captives and recovery of sight to the blind; to set free the oppressed and announce that the time has come when the Lord will save his people.' (Luke 4:18-19)

"After this, Jesus travelled in Galilee; he did not want to travel in Judea, because the Jewish authorities were wanting to kill him." (John 7:1)

"Then they picked up stones to throw at him, but Jesus hid himself and left the Temple." (John 8:58)

"When the people in the synagogue heard this, they were filled with anger. They rose up, dragged Jesus out of the town, and took him to the top of the hill on which their town was built. They meant to throw him over the cliff, but he walked through the middle of the crowd and went his way." (Luke 4:38-30)

"There was much whispering about him in the crowd. 'He is a good man', some people said. 'No', others said, 'he is misleading the people.' But no one talked about him openly, because they were afraid of the Jewish authorities." (John 7:12-13)

So yes, Jesus was most definitely politically active! And as such, he brought the wrath of the Jewish authorities down upon himself!

But there were others as well as Jesus causing trouble throughout the land!

There were the failed messiahs Theudas, 44 B.C.E., the Samaritan 36 C.E., and *'The Egyptian'*, 57 C.E., all of whom made messianic claims, and of course, Judas the Galilean who also failed. All of these are reported by Josephus, the only first-century Jewish historian, in his writings *'Jewish Antiquities'* and *'Jewish Wars'*.

According to Josephus:

"It came to pass, while Cuspius Fadus was procurator of Judea, that a certain charlatan, whose name was Theudas, persuaded a great part of the people to take their effects with them and follow him to

the Jordan river; for he told them he was a prophet and that he would, by his own command, divide the river, and afford them an easy passage over it. Many were deluded by his words. However, Fadus did not permit them to make any advantage of his wild attempt, but sent a troop of horsemen out against them. After falling upon them unexpectedly, they slew many of them, and took many of them alive. They also took Theudas alive, cut off his head, and carried it to Jerusalem. (Josephus: *Jewish Antiquities* 20.97-98)

The movement was dispersed and was never heard of again. Josephus does not provide a number for Theudas' followers, but Acts of the Apostles reports, when Peter and the apostles were being tried, that they numbered about 400:

"Gamaliel, who was a teacher of the Law and was highly respected by all the people, stood up in Council. He ordered the apostles to be taken out for a while. 'Fellow-Israelites, be careful what you do to these men. You remember that Theudas appeared some time ago, claiming to be somebody great, and about four hundred men joined him. But he was killed, all his followers scattered, and his movement died out. After that, Judas the Galilean appeared during the time of the census; he drew a crowd after him, but he also was killed, and all his followers were scattered.'" (Acts 5:34-37)

Judas of Galilee, or Judas of Gamala, was a Jewish leader who led resistance to the census imposed for Roman tax purposes by Quirinius in Judaea Province around 6 B.C.E. He encouraged Jews not to register and those who did had their houses burnt and their cattle stolen by his followers. He began *the 'Fourth Philosophy',* the *'Zealot'* movement which Josephus blames for the disastrous war with the Romans 66-70 C.E. They were called '*Zealots'* because of their intense *zeal* in pursuing their aims.

These events are all discussed by Josephus in '*The Jewish War*' and '*Antiquities*' and are also mentioned in the *Acts of the Apostles*.

When Paul was arrested in the Temple, the commander of the soldiers asked him:

'"'You speak Greek, do you?' the commander asked. Then you are not that Egyptian fellow who some time ago started a revolution and led four thousand armed terrorists out into the desert?' "* (Acts 21:37-38)

Acts explicitly states the Egyptian's followers were *sicarii,* the knife-wielding terrorists who assassinated Roman sympathisers. The Romans came to see any popular leader as a threat to their power, even Jesus and his followers.

"These deeds of the robbers filled the city with all sorts of impiety. And now conjurers and deceivers persuaded the multitude to follow them into the wilderness, and pretended that they would show them manifest wonders and signs that would be performed by the providence of God. And many that were persuaded suffered the pain of their folly, for Felix brought them back and punished them. At this time there came out of Egypt to Jerusalem a man who said he was a prophet, and advised the multitude of the common people to go along with him to the mountain called the Mount of Olives, which lay a distance of five furlongs from the city. He said that he would show them that at his command the walls of Jerusalem would fall down, through which he promised that he would procure them an entrance into the city. Now when Felix was informed of this he ordered his soldiers to take up their weapons, and with a great number of horsemen and footmen from Jerusalem he attacked the Egyptian and the people that were with him. He slew four hundred of them and took two hundred alive. But the

*Egyptian himself escaped from the fight and did not appear any
more. And again the robbers stirred up the people to make war
with the Romans."* (Antiquities 20.8.5 169-172   (War 2.13.5 261)

So there was what one could term a Jewish Freedom Movement at
the time of the birth of Jesus. And it was these who came to be
known as the Zealots. After the fall of Jerusalem in 70 C.E. what
remained of them fled to Masada, where they eventually took
their own lives rather than surrender to the Roman forces.
According to Josephus, our main, in fact our sole source for these
movements and consequences, their main characteristics were an
invincible love of freedom; a deep and bitter resentment of the
Roman census of Cyrenius, 6 C.E., which sparked off the revolt of
Judas of Galilee, and a profound belief that the people must co-
operate with God for his intervention and help.

Josephus seems to have had an ambivalent attitude towards the
Zealots. On the one hand, he appears to have considered them
dangerous fanatics, denigrating them as *'brigands'* yet on the other
hand, as a Jew himself, he could hardly fail to appreciate the fact
that they were dedicated to ridding the Jewish people of the
Roman oppressors together with their local representatives and
puppets. He refers to them as the *'Fourth Philosophy'* of the Jewish
people, the other three being the Pharisees, the Sadducees and
the Essenes. This *'Fourth Philosophy'* was founded by Judas the
Galilean in 6 C.E. and according to Josephus, *"all succeeding
troubles including the burning of the Temple can be traced to his
teaching."*

And of course, we cannot forget the Sicarii, the knife wielders! Yes,
Galilee was certainly a hot-bed! A political hot-bed!

So first-century Jewish Palestine was indeed a time and place of social unrest, political uprisings and insurrections that were brutally dealt with by the might of the Roman authorities. Certainly not the quiet, peaceful, tranquil life that has been depicted in the gospels, with Jesus and his disciples wandering casually from place to place, healing the sick and teaching freely in the Temple and in the synagogues.

And insurgents, Zealots and Sicarii were not the only ones who traversed through the Galilee region alongside Jesus and his disciples. There were others of a less aggressive nature out and about.

Many professional miracle workers and exorcists were plying their trade. Magic too was widely practised, for a fee.

"Many of those who had practised magic...." (Acts 19:19)

"..........where they met a certain magician named Bar-Jesus, a Jew who claimed to be a prophet......at once Elymas (that is his name in Greek) felt a dark mist cover his eyes....." (Acts 13:6-11)

"Now there was a certain man named Simon, who formerly was practising magic in the city, and astonishing the people of Samaria, claiming to be someone great; and they all, from smallest to greatest, were giving attention to him, saying, 'This man is what is called the Great Power of God. And they were giving him attention because he had for a long time astonished them with his magic arts." (Acts 8:9-11)

There were others. Honi ha-M'agel known as Honi the Circle-Drawer was, apparently, very adept at bringing on rain by drawing circles in the dust. He passed on his gifts to his grandsons, Abba Hilqiah and Hanan the Hidden, both of whom lived in Galilee at the time of Jesus.

Then there was Rabbi Hanina ben Dosa, who also possessed wonder working powers and was reported to pray over the sick and ward off death.

Apollonius of Tyana was another. A charismatic teacher and miracle-worker, he apparently healed the sick, cured the blind and the deaf, and is even reported as having raised a girl from the dead.

"One day, as we were going to the place of prayer, we were met by a young servant woman who had an evil spirit that enabled her to predict the future. She earned a lot of money for her owners by telling fortunes." (Acts 16:16)

Exorcists too abounded, probably the most famous one being Eleazar, thought to have been an Essene, the holy Jewish sect who were widely known for their healings and exorcisms. We read of many such exorcisms in the gospels.

And what about Jesus in all of this? Jesus was a Jew, not a Christian. A devout Jew, living in Roman occupied Judea in the first years of the first century C. E! And all Jews took their beliefs and responsibilities very seriously!

A Jewish father had five responsibilities towards his male offspring. Firstly, he had to have his newly-born son circumcised at the temple just eight days after he was born. Secondly, the parents of the child had to bring a sin offering to the temple. Wealthy parents would have brought a calf, sheep or goat, while poorer parents would have brought two doves. Joseph and Mary brought two doves:

"The time came for Joseph and Mary to perform the ceremony of purification, as the Law of Moses commanded. So they took the

child to Jerusalem to present him to the Lord, as it is written in the law of the Lord: 'Every firstborn male is to be dedicated to the Lord'. They also went to offer a sacrifice of a pair of doves or two young pigeons, as required by the law of the Lord". (Luke 2:22:24)

Thirdly, a Jewish father had to teach his son the Torah. The word Torah, as we have seen, was the Hebrew word for law, meaning direction, guidance and instruction, and included the books of Genesis, Exodus, Leviticus, Numbers and Deuteronomy. Fourthly, he had to teach his son a trade, so that when his son became an adult, he would in turn be able to support his own family. And fifthly, it was a Jewish father's responsibility to find a wife for his son before he was twenty years of age. Jews took the latter very seriously indeed!

In the book of Genesis it was written: "*He created them male and female, blessed them and said: 'Have many children so that your descendants will live all over the earth and bring it under their control.'* " (Genesis 1: 28)

And again: "*It is not good for the man to live alone*". (Genesis 2:18)

If a Jewish male reached twenty or beyond without being married, he would certainly have been looked upon with curiosity by the rest of his society, and his celibate state would have been a cause for much discussion and speculation, especially by those who may have been his enemies, and they would most certainly have used this against him.

There is no reference in any of the gospels as to whether Jesus was married or not. We know he was a member of the Essene Community, many of whom remained celibate, especially those who travelled around teaching, while others living at Qumran or at

Mount Carmel also often remained celibate. But there were those who married.

This Jewish race, to which Jesus belonged, believed God had chosen them to be his special people. They looked forward to the time when they would be restored to their former power and greatness and when all nations of the world would come to Jerusalem to worship in the Temple.

But instead, what was the situation in which they found themselves? What was their reality?

Here they were, forced to live in their own lands under the oppression of a foreign power, their religious customs insulted, false gods enforced upon them, offensive standards, flags and temples surrounding them. Even their own Temple changed into a model of that of Rome! And Herod the Great had not just confined his building extravaganza to Jerusalem! He had built a temple to the Roman Emperor in Caesarea, where, as in Jerusalem, he had built theatres and amphitheatres, and had introduced the games every fourth year in honour of Augustus. The naked competitors were greatly offensive to the Jews, as were the religious customs linked with the games. But the most offensive and despised of all was the eagle on the Temple in Jerusalem, the symbol of Roman power, dominating their city and seen for miles around. Roman soldiers were positioned on guard along all the main routes in and out of Jerusalem, more numerous at times of Jewish festivities, such as the politically sensitive Passover festival, when Jerusalem was thronged with Jews from all over the known world.

But it was the onerous, oppressive and excessive system of taxation, that was mostly the cause of unrest among the Jewish people. A Roman official, called a censor, was responsible for collecting the revenue from taxes. The censor sold the right to extort the payments to the highest bidder, and the successful appointee constantly demanded more than was due, pocketing the extra for himself.

According to Josephus, in Syria, one percent of a man's yearly income was paid in tax. On top of that, there were export and import duties, taxes on crops, which amounted to one tenth of the grain crop and one fifth of the wine and fruit, purchase taxes, taxes payable on transfer of property, taxes for carriage of goods on public highways and even emergency taxes.

So this was life in first-century Jewish Palestine!

Now it is time to consider another very important matter which was of paramount importance in setting the scene for the life of Jesus.

The Ancient Mystery Schools and the Ancient Mystery Teachings!

CHAPTER 7

THE ANCIENT MYSTERY SCHOOLS AND TEACHINGS

Many people today are completely unaware of the existence of the Ancient Mystery Schools as far back in history as over 4,000 years before the time of Yeshua, and continuing for several centuries after his death. History largely ignores these important establishments, in just the same way as the writers of all history choose what to include and what to leave out, depending on their own individual agenda.

But they definitely did exist, and in order to understand the life of Yeshua and his teachings, including all the wondrous deeds with which he has been credited, we need to look at these Ancient Mystery Schools more closely to ascertain the importance and relevance they exerted on the historical figure of Yeshua.

So what were these Ancient Mystery Schools? Where were they? What did they teach?

Based on deep philosophical thinkings, these Mystery Schools were developed in ancient times by the wise sages of many lands, supporting and guiding those who sought an alternative path to the shallow, artificial, destructive materialism of everyday living with its gross spiritual indifference, its superstitious ways, and its corrupt political and economic structures. They addressed the deeper meanings of existence, delving into the Spiritual world and into one's own inner Spiritual self for the answers to the deeper questions of life and death.

We know that Yeshua was teaching higher spiritual material than the ordinary people of his time were used to. We know too that he taught in parables to the crowds, while teaching the deeper knowledge to his disciples. And we know too that he has been unaccounted for by the gospels during his missing years, from he was twelve until he was about thirty and beginning his short ministry. Orthodox church teachings infer that when Jesus returned to Nazareth with his parents after he was found teaching in the temple at twelve years of age, he remained in Nazareth, learning and working as a carpenter like his father:

"So Jesus went back with them to Nazareth, where he was obedient to them. His mother treasured all these things in her heart. Jesus grew both in body and in wisdom, gaining favour with God and people." (Luke 32:51-52)

This is all the gospels tell us about Yeshua from he was twelve years of age until he began his ministry at the age of about thirty! Eighteen of the most formative years of Yeshua's life! And this is all we get?

The next we hear is that he is being baptised by John the Baptist, at thirty years of age. A changed Jesus from the last time we heard of him! Now a teacher, a healer, a man who demonstrated extraordinary powers, even over the elements.

And we know too that he raised many a Jewish eyebrow when he returned from wherever he was and began his teachings.

So where was he? Why do the gospels not tell us?

It is hardly credible that he spent them somewhere in hiding, away from the world! A twelve year old boy? So there must have been many people who knew exactly where he was and what he was doing. So why have the same people who gave us so much detail about his life in the gospels not included these missing years? They must have known! So why has it all been concealed? Or deliberately lost or wiped out?

Jesus growing up in Nazareth? Working as a carpenter with his father?

But! There are clues in the gospels which lead us to believe otherwise!

"He taught in the synagogues and was praised by everyone. Then Jesus went to Nazareth, where he had been brought up, and on the Sabbath he went as usual to the synagogue. He stood up to read the Scriptures and was handed the book of the prophet Isaiah. He unrolled the scroll and found the place where it is written : 'The Spirit of the Lord is upon me......................' Jesus rolled up the scroll, gave it back to the attendant, and sat down. All the people in the synagogue had their eyes fixed on him.........They were all well impressed with him and marvelled at the eloquent words that he spoke. They said, 'Isn't he the son of Joseph?'............Jesus said to them, 'I tell you this, prophets are never welcomed in their home town.' " (Luke 4:15-24)

Worthy of note here is that Jesus could read. Where did he learn that?

Worthy of note also is that these people did not recognise him! And these people lived in the small village of Nazareth! Where the gospels insinuate Jesus lived! A tiny hamlet, where everyone would have known everyone else and all about them!

And further of note, Jesus went to Nazareth, where *"he had been brought up".* This suggests he had been living elsewhere for a while. For eighteen years perhaps?

"He went as usual to the synagogue". But this does not automatically mean the Synagogue in Nazareth!

"Many people were there, and when they heard him, they were all amazed. 'Where did he get all this?' they asked. 'What wisdom is this that has been given him? How does he perform miracles? Isn't he the carpenter, the son of Mary; and the brother of James, Joseph, Judas, and Simon? Aren't his sisters living here?' And so they rejected him." (Mark 6:1-3)

The words *"Where did he get all this?"* certainly tell us that he did not get all this growing up in Nazareth! And why not? The most obvious conclusion must surely be, because he was not in Nazareth! If indeed, Nazareth itself even existed! Many scholars now claim that it did not! A made-up place-name for a made-up god-man!

"When Jesus finished telling these parables, he left that place and went back to his home town. He taught in the synagogue, and those who heard him were amazed. 'Where did he get such wisdom?' they asked. 'Isn't he the carpenter's son? Isn't Mary his mother, and aren't James, Joseph, Simon, and Judas his brothers? Aren't all his sisters living here? Where did he get all this?' And so they rejected him.

Jesus said to them, 'A prophet is respected everywhere except in his home town and by his own family.' Because they did not have faith, he did not perform many miracles there." (Matthew 13:53-58)

"The festival was nearly half over when Jesus went to the Temple and began preaching. The Jewish authorities were greatly surprised and said, 'How does this man know so much when he has never

had any training?' " (John 7:14-15)

And then there was the episode of the half-shekel temple tax which was levied on all male adults for the upkeep of the Temple and all who worked there:

"When Jesus and his disciples came to Capernaum, the collectors of the temple tax came to Peter and asked, 'Does your teacher pay the temple tax?'

"Of course', Peter answered.

When Peter went into the house, Jesus spoke up first, 'Simon, what is your opinion? Who pays duties or taxes to the kings of this world? The citizens of the country or the foreigners?'

'The foreigners,' answered Peter.

'Well, then,' replied Jesus, 'that means that the citizens don't have to pay. But we don't want to offend these people. So go to the lake and drop in a line. Pull up the first fish you hook, and in its mouth you will find a coin worth enough for my temple tax and yours. Take it and pay them our taxes.' " (Matthew 17:24027)

What significance can we attach to this?

Very simply, again, Jesus is not recognised by someone who should have been able to recognise him, if he had been there all those missing years. Jesus was frequently in Capernaum during his ministry, teaching and healing. If he had been in that area during those missing years, the Temple tax collector would certainly have known him. But here, he does not apparently know Jesus. And Jesus passes it all off in a humourous, light-hearted manner, describing himself as a foreigner in his own land!

And when Philip brought Nathaniel to meet Jesus:

"When Jesus saw Nathaniel coming to him, he said about him, 'Here is a real Israelite; there is nothing false in him!'

Nathaniel asked him, 'How do you know me?' " (John 1:47-48)

Nathaniel was from Cana, only about four miles north of the supposed Nazareth. Surely Nathaniel would have known Jesus, particularly through Jesus' teachings in the synagogue, if Jesus had been there all those missing years? Nathaniel obviously did not know Jesus or that he came from Nazareth.

There is only one possible conclusion! Jesus had not been in Nazareth during those missing years!

So where was he?

Wherever he was, he must have learned to read and write and to know the scriptures and the laws in great detail, because when he came back, he astounded them all with his knowledge.

And his teachings were so contradictory to the beliefs of the Jewish people and so unacceptable, even so offensive to them that his life was in danger, so therefore he could not have gained all his knowledge, learning and healing skills in any place where the Jewish religion was established.

Finally, there is no reference in any of the canonical gospels to Jesus being married. Now we know that those canonical gospels were deliberately chosen by a male dominated group of people, church fathers, gathered together for the purpose of putting some structure on the fledgling new Christian Church, and keeping Jesus celibate for their own obvious reason. But still, when we take this all into account, we must also remember that the Torah instructed that all young Jewish males were to be married by the age of twenty, and if not, it would have been a matter of conjecture and curiosity as to why not. Jesus returns at the age of thirty from wherever he was, with totally different views from the Torah, especially on the role and importance of women, and he included many women in his ministry. Where did he get these ideas?

So, where was he?

Wherever he was, it was there he gained Enlightenment, it was there he reached Awareness, it was there he accessed his Christ Consciousness, it was there he achieved self-mastery. It was there he discovered his own divinity, his own connection to the Infinite.

The activities and whereabouts of Jesus before the start of his ministry at the age of thirty have been the subject of much speculation. Some scholars suggest he travelled far beyond the boundaries of Palestine in his search for Spiritual knowledge and wisdom. India? Britain? The East? Elizabeth Clare Prophet, in her book 'The Lost Years of Jesus', documents evidence of Jesus' 17-year journey to the East.

Let us return now to those ancient Mystery Schools, because it is those very same ancient Mystery Schools and their teachings that hold the key to Jesus' missing years!

So what were these Mystery Schools? What were they teaching? How was this esoteric, inner knowledge passed on?

Today, most people are oblivious to the fact that all forms of life in the entire cosmos are connected. Many people simply exist on the material level, believing that this physical world is the centre of everything, the most important planet in existence. But there are others who know the truth. There are others who know that we here on Planet Earth are merely a small grain of sand in the entirety of all the universes in the totality of creation. There are those who know that the only difference between our small planet and all the other planets and universes is that we are all operating on different energy vibrational levels and that those different energy vibrational levels can be crossed by those who know how.

And there are those who know that we are all connected in the great universal Oneness of the entirety of creation. The microcosmic energy systems of the earth are interconnected with the vast macrocosmic systems of the stellar matrix, all held together by the most exquisite, the most intricate, the most ingenious of geometrical designs and mathematical equations, heaven-and-earth alignments and sonar sound vibrations of, for example, the dolphins and whales.

But of course, all this knowledge is not available to the masses! Students in schools everywhere are taught mathematics and geometry, how to work out various mathematical and geometric equations, but they are not taught that it is mathematical equations and geometrical designs that hold entire creation together! Nor are they taught about the sonar sounds emitted by dolphins and whales and how they too hold creation together! Nor are they taught about all the subtle energy fields surrounding each and every one of us, the energetic pathways of our own human physical bodies, accessible through our inner Spiritual Chakra system, or the energetic ley-lines of the earth.

And why, we may well ask, do our education systems not teach all this?

The answer is obvious! In order to be controlled, we need to be kept in the dark, in ignorance, by those who seek to take our power away from us and manipulate us for their own devious and mercenary ends. We need to be kept dependent on external forces and authorities and not ever allowed access to our own inherent divine nature where we find within ourselves all the answers to all the questions we could ever ask and where we have unlimited potentiality. If this were ever to happen, as indeed it will, if there comes a time, as indeed there will, when we can access our own inherent divine potentiality, then those powers are defunct, obsolete, no longer in control. We are kept under control by the belief that we are sinners, so far below Jesus that we will never get to where he is, and that the church is our only means of salvation. That's it in a nutshell!

The early Christian Church based its teachings and dogmas on its own version of what they decided were to be the canonical gospels, instead of the real teachings of Yeshua, which were in their turn based on the teachings of the ancient Mystery Schools.

Jesus himself upbraided the teachers of the Law:

"How terrible for you teachers of the Law! You have kept the key that opens the door to the house of knowledge; you yourselves will not go in, and you stop those who are trying to go in!" (Luke 11:52)

But in the time of Yeshua, and for over 4,000 years before that, these ancient Mystery Schools were the teachers of accessing other worlds and energy vibrational levels. But they were not called '*Mystery Schools*' for nothing! They were secretive, mostly passing their teachings down orally, and not written, in order to protect that secrecy, and to ensure that the knowledge did not pass into the wrong hands. And this esoteric, inner knowledge was passed down through symbols. The Gospel of Philip, not included in the canonical gospels confirms this:

'The mysteries of Truth are manifested to us in the form of

archetypes or images.' (Gospel of Philip, Plate 132)

And of course, we all know that the ancient Egyptians communicated through symbols in their hieroglyphics, their system of writing and communication where pictures and symbols represented a word or sound. And the Egyptians, as we also know, were deeply ensconced in the ancient Mystery Schools and Mystery Teachings.

Hitler knew well the importance and significance of sacred symbols. He inverted one of the most ancient of sacred symbols, the Antakarana into his Swastika symbol which he used to terrorise Europe. Virgin Atlantic Airlines has the sacred inclusive symbol of the Lemniscate, the figure eight, on the tail of all its aircraft. Most advertisements that flash across our television screens now feature spirals, circles or triangles, all various and diverse aspects of cosmic geometry. And Feng Shui, as we all know, is the art of using the earth's energy lines to build houses and to place objects in a particular position to maximise the natural energy coming from the earth and from surrounding energy fields.

When we talk about *'Enlightened Beings',* we mean those souls amongst us who have already achieved a high degree of Spiritual awareness, raised Spiritual consciousness, Spiritual Enlightenment. These beings exist in the upper echelons of the hierarchy of the Spirit worlds, but they are not detached from us, by any means. Remember! We are all connected! We are all connected right across the entire plethora of the different vibrational energy levels throughout the entire spectrum of creation. These already Enlightened beings are no different from us, except that they are further along the path to Enlightenment, and, acknowledging the inter-connectedness of all forms of life, they are devoted to supporting us and helping us attain what they have already attained.

Their influence and inspiration manifest constantly on this material earth plane. Where, for example, do you think all the great scientific discoveries originate? All the great musical masterpieces? All the great art and sculpture works? All the new technological wonders? Yes, they all originate in the soul of each individual genius, but remember, the soul is the part of each of us connected to the higher vibrational energy levels. Our soul, depending on its present state of awareness, its present level of raised energy vibration, is either able or not able to receive these transmissions, *"He that hath ears to hear!"* And then these transmissions manifest on this dense energy earth plane. So everything, absolutely everything starts in the Spiritual energy fields, in a higher vibrational frequency, and descends through the mental and the emotional to the physical.

So exactly who are we talking about here? Can we name any of these already Enlightened beings who continue to reach out to us here on Planet Earth, trying to awaken us and raise our Spiritual consciousness?

Well, we have Buddha; Zoroaster of Persia; Lao Tzu of China; the mysterious Magi, fathers of astronomy; Hippocrates, father of modern medicine; Euclid, father of geometry; Pythagoras, father of mathematics; Democritus, father of the atom. Plus, of course, the great philosophers like Pluto, Plato, Thales, Socrates, Aristotle, Heraclitus and many more. All of these were initiates of the ancient Mystery Traditions.

And all down through history, they continue to inspire and influence us here on Planet Earth. Leonardo da Vinci, Isaac Newton, Roger Bacon, William Wordsworth, Walter Raleigh, John

Milton, Thomas More, Copernicus, Galileo, William Blake, Botticelli, Victor Hugo, - all have been learned initiates from the ancient Mystery Traditions. All have been at a sufficiently raised soul awareness level to be able to receive and absorb the transmissions from the higher Spiritual energy levels.

The over-seeing mystical body that supports all of these is known in the higher Spiritual echelons as The Great White Brotherhood, or the mystical Fellowship of Light. These are those highly evolved Enlightened Spiritual beings who, from time to time, reincarnate here on Planet Earth to help us ascend the cosmic escalator to a higher energy vibrational frequency. These are the holy sages, the teachers, the masters, the adepts, of every nationality and race, who have attained Spiritual Enlightenment and who are now devoted to uplifting humanity to a higher Spiritual consciousness, and to awaken us all from our long slumber, in this time of the Great Awakening following the 2012 re-alignment of the planets, allowing unprecedented mass higher energies to flood Planet Earth as never before.

Here too were to be found the Freemasons, the Rosicrucians, the Theosophists, the Knights Templar, the Cathars, The Knights of the Round Table, all of whom have been persecuted and exterminated by religious authorities down through history, simply because they carried the seeds of truth from the ancient Mystery Schools, truths which had to be exterminated at all costs by those who sought power over the masses.

And they were greatly assisted in that extermination by the rapid decline in virtue, morality and spirituality, a decline which has preceded the destruction of every nation in history. When a nation loses its spirituality, its connection to the whole, its connection to Source, it rapidly declines. The ancient mysteries through time became perverted, those secret societies became infiltrated, sorcery and black witchcraft replacing the divine magic. Hence, today, we have only murmerings of those ancient mysteries remaining.

The adepts and sages of the ancient Mystery Schools fully understood that beneath the world of the five physical senses lies a vastly greater Universal Intelligence. The Roman Catholic Church equally understands that knowledge such as these ancient teachers possessed is a threat to their power and authority, should it ever leak out and ooze down to the masses. Hence the history of the Roman Catholic Church is permeated with violence, persecution and murder, all in order to destroy all those who could possibly be a threat to their control of all of humanity's financial and energetic resources. The distortion by these same so-called Christian hierarchies of the knowledge and teachings of the ancient Mystery Schools was deliberately undertaken in order to consolidate its political, financial and religious power over the masses through brandishing the double-barrelled weapon of fear and guilt.

But Yeshua himself was an initiate of these Mystery Schools, and his teachings were deeply embedded into his ministry! Is it not obvious then, why the Christian Church has deliberately erased Jesus' connections to the ancient Mysteries? Is it not obvious why the canonical gospels, as presented to us by the Christian Church, completely fail to mention these ancient mysteries? All in an attempt to make sure that no-one hears about them and therefore, no-one can follow in Jesus' footsteps! The stark message is being delivered! No-one can stand outside the control of the Church!

And this from the same Christian Church that proclaims itself to be the one and only true church based on the teachings of Jesus!

Remind me again what Leonardo da Vinci said!

'Blinding ignorance does mislead us. O wretched mortals, open your eyes!'

The reasons for secrecy on the part of the Church are totally different from the reasons for secrecy by the ancient sages and adepts!

The ancient holders of the knowledge of the mysteries kept everything secret out of respect for that sacred knowledge, and to prevent it from falling into the wrong hands. They understood fully the disastrous effect the mastery of natural forces such as electricity, atomic power and magnetism would have for Planet Earth and indeed the entire Cosmos should such knowledge be usurped and fall into the wrong hands. The Christian Church hierarchies, however, have kept all this sacred knowledge secret in order to maintain their power, and retain control.

While the ancient Mystery Schools allowed only the most trustworthy and tested students access to this sacred knowledge, and that only after a long period of probationship, the Roman Catholic hierarchy have gained their positions right down through history by simony, bribery and political intrigue.

Those people who today work in the areas of holistic healing, Reiki and Celestial energies, integrated therapies, are familiar with names such as Saint Germaine, Serapis Bey, Lantos, and the Supreme Masters such as Jesus, known in the higher planes as Sananda; Babaji; Thoth; Quan Yin, Isis; Kumara, to mention but a few.

So what was taught in these great Mystery Schools of Greece and

India, so strongly connected with the Essenes and the Egyptian Therapeutae?

There were usually three progressive and intense stages of learning, beginning with the Lesser Mysteries, then the Greater Mysteries, and culminating in Mastery.

The Lesser Mysteries concentrated on the whole meaning of life, the nature of life and death, the purpose of man's existence, the inter-connectedness of all forms of life in the great Universal Energy that encompasses all things. The Oneness of all creation and the Laws of Karma were all taught through the study of the movement of the stars and planets and the energy pathways of the chakra system of the human body in alignment with the energy ley-lines of the earth and the energy vibrational frequencies of entire creation. Sciences, mathematics and geometry instilled an understanding of the mechanics of the universe. The whole meaning and working of energy was mastered at this first level, with the student taught how to work within subtle energy fields; how energy attracts like energy and hence the importance of our complete awareness of every thought and word we send out into the universe and into the vast energy network surrounding us on all sides, and how we can control what happens within those subtle energy fields for the good of mankind. And that was the reason for all the secrecy surrounding this sacred knowledge, and ensuring it would not fall into the wrong hands! It could also be used for destruction!

At this first level, the student was also taught to realise his own divine nature and unlimited potentiality. He was taught how to transcend this material physical world, like in near-death experiences and to return to the physical body before the silver cord disconnected, that spiritual cord that connects the soul to the physical body, in just the same way as the umbilical cord connects the babe in the womb to the mother, and is disconnected after birth.

Today, we see this same ability to move in and out of other worlds and vibrational energy levels practised by Shamans and Mystics. I saw myself, in Bali, how young men could induce a deep trance state through dance, and then transcend any physical manifestation of injury or pain inflicted on their bodies, such as knife wounds.

First level students also studied the balance of mind, body and spirit through meditation, toning and chanting, tantric arts or internal energy practices, yogic positions and inter-dimensional contact; biology; botany; healing with herbs; hands-on healing and naturopathy. The supreme teacher was Nature, and close observation of Nature was vital for learning the natural laws and understanding the Divine Feminine. The right and left Eye of Horus were mastered, the right eye representing the masculine and the left eye the feminine.

The Essenes, as we shall see in a later chapter, with whom Jesus was closely connected, were initiated in all of this. Jesus employed these practices when he cast out devils, healed the sick, controlled the forces of nature and even foretold his own crucifixion.

Certainly a lot for first-level students!

Having mastered the Lesser Mysteries, the student then progressed to the Greater Mysteries.

Here the Divine Masculine was understood. Also the importance of dying to the ego. Of special significance was the learning of spiritual journeys into non-ordinary states of reality, where the student was led through a death-and rebirth process by being taken, blind-folded, through a series of dark caves or underground passages, where they were forced to confront their deepest fears and where they came into contact through visions, with other higher vibrational energy level entities. Initiates of the Mystery Schools discovered for themselves the secrets of life, death and rebirth. So they saw there was nothing to fear from death.

We have examples of this in Claire Heartsong's book 'Anna, Grandmother of Jesus', where Yeshua himself was led through just such an experience at twelve years of age in Mount Carmel, in what was called the Rite of the Sepulchre, where Jesus experienced the ancient ritual of 'dying' and resurrection. And later, on Mount Sinai, Yeshua experienced another initiation. Led blindfolded to the highest crags and left alone without food or water for four days and nights, he was instructed to remain within the circumference of a small circle and to find shelter amongst the stones. He walked in a circular motion while meditating, weaving patterns of sacred geometry, enduring the blazing furnace of the sun during the day and the freezing cold at night. This was, again, an initiation process, where he was exposed to the elements, the four-legged and winged creatures and the demonic and higher celestial energy forces that presented themselves to him in visions and dreams.

Further such initiations were undergone by Yeshua in Egypt, this time in the Great Pyramid at Giza, in dark, deep underground passages, again described in detail in Claire Heartsong's book, where Yeshua's Spiritual consciousness was further refined, opened to the subtle energies of the mystic, higher realms, and his constitution and character strengthened. The Great Pyramid, described by Heartsong as *"far from serving as a monumental tomb for one of the ancient Egyptian pharaohs, the Great Pyramid was and is, not only an initiation chamber, but also an extraordinarily powerful ascension chamber. It was designed to help initiates awaken to the full remembrance of their true identity. This is the secret of the pyramid."* ('Anna, Grandmother of Jesus' Chapter 32 Page 241)

So these Greater Mysteries taught about the seven dimensional levels of reality, explored the vast cycles of time that govern human evolution and knowledge of worlds within the universe. Physicists today are just rediscovering these multi-dimensional realms that lie beyond our physical senses, but they were known to the mystics of virtually every spiritual tradition in the ancient world.

Finally, the Mastery. This was all about achieving awareness of both the male and female aspects of the Divine, bringing integration and personal balance, which was vital and fundamental to becoming Enlightened. We all have both feminine and masculine aspects to us, having spent numerous life-times as both male and female, balancing these energies within our soul. After becoming integrated and balanced, initiates then committed themselves to the Enlightenment of others. They literally died to their old way, passing beyond surface illusions to the heart of their own divine essence and returned transformed.

"Most assuredly, I say to you, unless you be born again, you cannot see the kingdom of God." (John 3:3)

So in these ancient teachings, the Divine Feminine was extolled, respected and revered. Unfortunately, however, our present-day culture denigrates the Divine Feminine so we have lost the ancient ability to balance the masculine and feminine energies that is required on the earth plane, with the result that our world has thus been out of balance for many centuries. There must be a balance, as in the Gospel of Philip we read: "*Truth is the Mother; knowledge is the Father......*"

And what, if anything at all, do the early writers, philosophers and historians tell us about these Ancient Mysteries?

"*While we are encumbered by bodily affections, we can have no intercourse with God..... But when our souls are released (by the Mysteries) and have passed into the region of the pure, invisible and changeless, this God will be our guide and king.....*" (Plutarch, the Greek historian 46-120 C.E.)

Plato also writes of a "*divine initiation*" through which aspirants "*become spectators of single and blessed visions, residents in a pure light, and are made immaculate and liberated from this surrounding garment which we call the body.....*"

As the ancient city of Athens declined, Alexandria was developing on the southern shore of the Mediterranean. In 331 B.C.E. Alexander the Great re-incarnated the spirit of Greece and Athens within his new university in Alexandria. His ancestor, the first Ptolemy, had been a student of Aristotle, and now Grecian, Roman, Persian, Babylonian, Hindu and Jewish teachings and writings were all contained within Alexandria. The works of Homer, Plato, Pythagoras, Aeschylus, Sophocles, Euripides and Aristotle were all available to the great numbers of students who studied and translated the ancient texts. Teachers and students were drawn from across the Eastern worlds, uniting the philosophies of the East and West.

As the larger Mystery Schools gradually declined, they were replaced by smaller '*gnostic*' groups, each of them specialising in keeping alive some special phase of the '*gnosis'*, meaning '*ancient knowledge'*.

In Ephesus, Buddhism, Zoroastrianism and the Chaldean system were taught along with the Platonic philosophy, while in Aegea, another gnostic school taught the doctrines of Pythagoras. In Egypt, many of the gnostic schools were affiliated with Judaism, and the Egyptian Mysteries were being perpetuated by the Essenes in their '*lesser'* and '*greater'* mysteries. There was also a Pythagorean branch of the Essenes, known as the '*Koinobi'*, as well as the Gymnosophists, while in Egypt, in Alexandria, the Pythagorean group were known as the '*Therapeutae'*.

And indeed, we do not have to go to Egypt and Greece to find these ancient Mystery Schools! We have similar nearer to home! We have the Celtic Druids! All equally ensconced in the ancient Mysteries as the Essenes, with whom Jesus was so strongly connected, and the Egyptian Therapeutae.

The Druids, it is generally accepted, were direct descendants from those who survived the fall of the ancient continent of Atlantis. Druidic Mystery Schools provided a system of education far in advance of their contemporaries in the rest of the then known continent of Europe, and hence Gallic students sought philosophical learning and training at the Druid Schools in Britain. These too were cloaked in secrecy, like the ancient Mystery Schools of Greece and Egypt, the knowledge being handed down orally to specially prepared and tested candidates, in order to protect it from falling into the wrong hands.

Scholars differ in where this Druidic Mysteries originated. Some speculate that the Druidic priests obtained their wisdom from Phoenician and Tyrian sea navigators visiting the Isles of Britain thousands of years before the time of Jesus, searching for tin. Joseph of Arimathea, an uncle of Jesus, as we have already seen, is widely reported to have been engaged in the tin mining trade, frequently visiting Britain and procuring vast amounts of tin for the Roman armies. It is widely reported that the young Jesus made frequent trips with his uncle, spending time being initiated into the Druidic Mysteries. Other scholars maintain that Druidic Mysteries were of Oriental origin, possibly Buddhistic.

Before a candidate was admitted and instructed in the secret doctrines of the Druids, he was sworn to secrecy, the teachings and knowledge being imparted only in deep forests and dark caves. Here, far from other men, the student was instructed in the creation of the universe, the laws of nature, the secrets of medicine, the mysteries of the celestial bodies, and magic and sorcery.

Like nearly all schools of the Ancient Mysteries, the teachings of the Druids were divided into distinct phases. The most simple of these teachings, a moral code, was taught to all the people, while the deeper, esoteric, inner doctrines were reserved for only initiated priests. A candidate had to be from a reputable family and of high moral character, and no important secret teachings were entrusted to him until he had passed various tests of temptation and strength of character. The Druids taught the immortality of the soul, transmigration of soul between worlds and reincarnation, as well as the Laws of Karma, cause and effect. They had a deep understanding of Nature and her laws. They studied geography, physical science, natural theology and astrology. They had a fundamental knowledge of medicine, especially the use of herbs and plants. They cured by magnetism and charging amulets and jewellery with healing energies.

The first known text that describes the Druids is Julius Caesar's *Commentarii de Bello Gallico* Book vi, written in the 50s or 40s B.C.E. A military general who was intent on conquering Gaul and Britain, Caesar described the Druids as being concerned with *"divine worship, the due performance of sacrifices, private or public, and the interpretation of ritual questions."*

Caesar claimed that the Druids played an important part in Gaulish society and that they performed the function of judges. They viewed Britain as the centre of Druidic learning, and students had to learn all the Druidic lore by heart. Their main teaching, according to Caesar, was that *"souls do not perish, but after death pass from one to another".* They were also concerned with *"the stars and their movements, the size of the cosmos and the earth, the world of nature, and the powers of deities."*

"It is they who decide in almost all disputes, public and private; and if any crime has ben committed, or murder done, or there is any dispute about succession or boundaries, they also decide it, determining rewards and penalties: if any person or people does not abide by their decision, they ban such from sacrifice, which is their heaviest penalty." (Caesar: 'Gallic Wars')

"A great number of young men gather about them for the sake of instruction and hold them in great honour.......Report says that in the schools of the Druids they learn by heart a great number of verses, and.........they do not think it proper to commit these utterances to writing, although in almost all other matters, and in their public and private accounts, they make use of Greek letters". (Caesar: 'Gallic Wars')

Other classical writers also commented on the Druids and their practices. Cicero, for example, a contemporary of Caesar's, commented on how the Druids knew much about the natural world and performed divination.

Diodorus Siculus, writing about 36 B.C.E. viewed the Druids as philosophers and theologians, with many poets and songsters in Celtic society, called *'bards'*.

Tacitus, the Roman writer, a senator and historian, described how in a battle against the Romans when the Romans attacked Anglesey, the Druids, with hands uplifted towards the sky, poured down such torrents of curses and *"terrible imprecations"* on the heads of the invaders. He states that these *"terrified our soldiers who had never seen such a thing before..."*

The Druids included philosophers, theologians, priests, judges, guarantors of political institutions, educators of the young and magicians. And it is clear from most sources that the Druids were teachers, teaching at both an esoteric and exoteric level. Their teachings were based on the five elements: earth, sea, sky, sun and moon. They were also seers and wonderworkers, of unusual skills.

"Some say that the study of philosophy was of barbarian origin. For the Persians had their Magi, the Babylonians or the Assyrians the Chaldeans, the Indians their Gymnosophists, while the Kelts and the Galatae had seers called Druids....." (Diogenes Laertius: 'Lives of the Philosophers' circa 250 C.E.)

A Druid usually had one or more students living in his household, in just the same as a Jewish Rabbi would have had a Talmudic School. It is recorded that in Ulster, Cathbad, the chief Druid at the court of King Conor MacNeasa had over one hundred students at any one time. The relationship between the king and Druid was of extreme importance. The Druid's favourite tree was the Rowan tree, for it was under the Rowan tree that he would sleep, in order to gain prophetic visions from his dreams.

Students in the Druidic schools were taught philosophy, law, magic, healing skills, divination, the sciences, chemistry, alchemy, astronomy, astrology, mathematics and numerology. The stone circles that they built required exact and sophisticated measuring, calculating and engineering skills and depended upon a deep knowledge of the movement of the planets. It was their knowledge and skill in astronomy that enabled them to build Newgrange and Stonehenge, the same skills that enabled the pyramids in Egypt to be built.

A number of legends suggest that Jesus travelled to the British Isles, to the lands of the Druids and the Celts, in the company of his uncle, Joseph of Arimathea, the wealthy tin merchant. Gordon Strachan's book on Mystery Religion and Knowledge uncovered a fascinating network of connections between the Celtic world and Mediterranean culture and philosophy. It was his book that was the basis for the film documentary 'And did those feet', which screened at the BFI in London in 2010. The title is taken from the famous poem, 'Paracelus', written by the mystic poet William Blake in 1805:

"And did those feet in ancient time / Walk upon England's mountain green? / And was the Holy Lamb of God / On England's pleasant pastures seen? / And did the Countenance Divine / Shine forth upon our clouded hills? / And was Jerusalem builded here / Among these dark, satanic mills?"

The 'dark satanic mills' is a reference to the Industrial Revolution, where machines replaced manual work and the factories belched out dark smoke through their chimneys.

Archaeologist and classical scholar Dennis Price, in his book 'The

Missing Years of Jesus', after a lengthy investigation into the myths and legends of Avalon and Glastonbury, offers extraordinary evidence that Jesus did indeed visit the British Isles with Joseph of Arimathea. And further substantial investigation is offered in George Jowett's book *'The Drama of the Lost Disciples'.*

So, if Jesus did indeed spend time with the Druids and Celts, and it is not for me to say whether he did or did not, then what could he have learned there?

"When the people in the synagogue heard this, they were filled with anger. They rose up, dragged Jesus out of the town, and took him to the top of the hill on which their town was built. They meant to throw him over the cliff, but he walked through the middle of the crowd and went his way." (Luke 4:28-30)

"Once more they tried to seize Jesus, but he slipped out of their hands." (John 10:39)

Well this certainly gives us food for thought!

Could this mean that Jesus was able to make himself invisible when necessary? To pass through crowds unseen?

The Druids were, as we know, descendants of those of Atlantis who had escaped the flood, in particular those who moved to Egypt and then moved progressively westwards. The civilisation that was Atlantis had powers and technology far beyond our present understanding or even our imagination. They could bi-locate, tele-port, travel long distances by a sort of bounding movement where their feet did not make contact with the ground, mind read and foretell the future. Certainly, these skills and qualities were carried down through the ages through the Druids and the ancient Mystery Schools.

And 2,000 years ago, it was in the gnostic schools, all of which were remnants of the Ancient Mystery Schools, that Jesus received his knowledge and was initiated into the ancient rites. He was definitely initiated into the secrets of the Egyptian Mysteries through the Pythagorean branch of the Essenes, evidenced by the fact that most of the teachings attributed to Jesus are in the Pythagorean spirit.

So the Essene Brotherhood did indeed have its roots firmly grounded in the ancient Mystery Schools. They were a Jewish sect representing an esoteric aspect of Judaism or Jewish mysticism.

Yes, Jesus' teachings were built around the ancient mysteries and initiations!

And we find clear mention and references to all this in the other gospels found at Nag Hammadi, and not included in the canonical gospels. In the Gospel of Thomas we read:

"It is to those who are worthy of my mysteries that I tell my mysteries."

The Gospel of Philip, a collection of Jesus' sayings that focus on the four great sacramental mysteries of Christianity,- baptism, anointing, the Eucharist and the Bridal Chamber, reports Jesus as saying:

"Those above, revealed to those below, so that we could know the mysteries of Truth."

Again, Philip writes: *"The Master did everything in a mystery; (his rites of passage were) baptism, chrism, Eucharist, redemption, and bridal chamber",* referring to the Mysteries' initiatory rites of being born, committing to the Divine, sacrificing to unconditional love, surrendering to grace and finally embracing the *"sacred marriage"* between the inner male and female.

And, of course, the early church fathers knew all about them! Clement of Alexandria, one of these early church fathers, described a secret gospel of Mark:

"It is a more spiritual gospel, read only to those who are being initiated into the Great Mysteries."

We have already seen how Jesus himself taught in parables. Where did he learn that?

The use of parable, story and myth was a powerful teaching device employed by the Egyptian Schools, whose initiates even encoded their hieroglyphic writings on three different levels, so they could be understood by all, delivering different meanings depending on the reader's level of esoteric training.

And Jesus was taught in those Egyptian schools!

So we can clearly see that a lot has been left out of Western Christianity about Jesus' participation in the mystery traditions.

Jesus was trained in the Mysteries. His life and miracles, which were performed in accordance with natural law, show that he had discovered the invisible secrets behind the world of form and matter.

Whether he was born with these gifts or acquired them through study does not matter. Only a highly advanced soul could have achieved this level of balance and integration. Not all of the Essenes could operate at this level, only those at the very highest amongst their progressive ranks. And Jesus was one such!

Origen, an early church father, writing some 200 years after the death of Jesus, writes again of the secret mysteries. He calls the faith of the masses *"somnatic Christianity",* and he separates this common faith from a higher wisdom founded on a genuine experience of the inner planes and a knowledge of cosmic law.

So it is clear that there was once a legacy of mystery teachings within the early Christian movement and these mysteries were more than likely taught by Jesus. But, they have been lost for over 1,600 years.

Jesus clearly spent time learning at these ancient Mystery Schools, in Egypt and with the Druids in Britain.

So although many of us proclaim to be Christian, the fact is that we really know very little about the ancient wisdom that lies at the core of our existence. And what does that say about us? The same way that most of us have never read the gospels! We have just taken what was handed out to us in Church teachings as the inspired word of God!

This ancient wisdom that has been kept from us for over 2,000 years!

So now that we have considered the setting and background to the life of Yeshua, let us now look at the plot and script for that same drama.

The prophecies of the Old Testament!

CHAPTER 8

PLOT AND SCRIPT: The prophecies of the Old Testament

All Jewish people were familiar with and knew well the ancient prophecies in the Old Testament about how God was coming to rescue his chosen people from the oppression of the foreign invaders, the Romans, through a Messiah who would be born to them.

As we have seen, the society into which Jesus was born was awash with self-proclaimed Messianic preachers travelling the entire country, all claiming to be the expected Messiah, and all raising the hopes and expectations of the Jewish nation suffering under Roman oppression.

The Old Testament includes over fifty different clear prophecies of the coming of the Messiah, with over three hundred references, all indicating to the Israeli people how they would be able to recognise the Messiah when he did come.

And all the different fractious sects in Jewish Palestine, including the Pharisees, the Sadducees, the Essenes, the Zealots, seemed to have a different expectation of what exactly the Messiah would be like.

Some expected a fighter who would lead an armed insurrection and rid Israel of the hated Romans and their hated puppet Jewish authorities. Others expected a king who would annihilate the present world and build a new, peaceful world from among the ruins. Yet others saw him as a prophet or priest who would restore, in some way, the Jews to their previous positions of power and glory.

Jesus, throughout the canonical Gospels, several times says that he is fulfilling a prophecy of the Old Testament. For example, in Luke's Gospel, after his Resurrection, he told his disciples: *"These are the very things I told you about while I was still with you: everything written about me in the Law of Moses, the writings of the prophets, and the Psalms had to come true............This is what was written: 'The Messiah must suffer and must rise from death three days later, and in his name the message about repentance and the forgiveness of sins must be preached to all nations, beginning in Jerusalem'."* (Luke: 24:44-47)

Again*: "If you had really believed Moses, you would have believed me, because he wrote about me".* (John 5: 46)

So here we have clear indications, from the Gospels, that Jesus knew about the prophecies in the Old Testament.

And of course, we have the constant repetition right through the canonical gospels of words like:

"But the Scriptures must come true." (Mark 14:49)

"For the Scripture says...." (Matthew 4:6)

"This was done to make what the prophet Isaiah had said come true." (Matthew 4:14)

"This, however was bound to happen so that what is written in their Law may come true." (John 15:24)

"Now all this happened in order to make what the Lord said through the prophets come true." (Matthew 1:22)

"But in that case, how could the Scriptures come true, which say that this is what must happen?" (Matthew 26:54)

""But all this has happened in order to make what the prophets wrote in the Scriptures come true." (Matthew 26: 56)

Let us now look at some of these prophecies, with which Jesus was apparently familiar! And at how they came to be fulfilled! And especially at the prophecies concerning his suffering and supposed death, as this is what we are mainly concerned with in this book.

Prophecy: The Messiah would be hated for no reason: "*Those who hate me for no reason are more numerous than the hairs of my head; My enemies tell lies against me; they are strong and want to kill me*". (Psalms 69:4)

This was fulfilled: "*If the world hates you, just remember that it hated me first...... they have seen what I did and they hate both me and my father. This, however, was bound to happen so that what is written in their Law may come true: They hated me for no reason at all*". (John 15:18)

Prophecy: The Messiah will enter Jerusalem on a donkey: "*Look, your king is coming to you! He comes triumphant and victorious; but humble and riding on a donkey, on a colt, the foal of a donkey*". (Zechariah 9:9)

This was fulfilled: "*......and they took the colt to Jesus. Then they threw their cloaks over the animal and helped Jesus get on. As he rode on, people spread their cloaks on the road*". (Luke 19:35)

Prophecy: The Messiah would be betrayed by a friend: "*Even my best friend, the one I trusted most, the one who shared my food, has turned against me*". (Psalms 41:9)

This was fulfilled, when Jesus responded to the traitor's kiss from Judas, saying to him: *"Be quick about it, friend!"* (Matthew 26:50) and again: *"When Judas, the traitor, learnt that Jesus had been condemned, he repented and took back the 30 silver coins to the chief priests and the elders. 'I have sinned by betraying an innocent man to death!' he said".* (Matthew 27: 3-4)

Prophecy: The Messiah would be betrayed for 30 pieces of silver: *"So they paid me 30 pieces of silver as my wages".* (Zechariah 11:12)

This was fulfilled: *"He (Judas) took back the 30 silver coins to the chief priests and the elders".* (Matthew 27:3)

Prophecy: The Messiah would not defend himself: *"He was treated harshly, but endured it humbly; he never said a word. Like a lamb about to be slaughtered, like a sheep about to be sheared, he never said a word".* (Isaiah 53:7)

This was fulfilled: *"But he said nothing in response to the accusations of the chief priests and elders.............but Jesus refused to answer a single word".* (Matthew 27:12; 27:14)

Prophecy: the Messiah will be beaten and spat upon: *"I bared my back to those who beat me. I did not stop them when they insulted me....... and spat in my face".* (Isaiah 50:6)

This was fulfilled: *"Then they spat in his face and beat him".* (Matthew 26:67)

Prophecy: The Messiah will say: *"My God, my God, why have you abandoned me?"* (Psalms 22:1)

This was fulfilled: *"Jesus cried out with a loud voice: My God, my God, why do you abandon me?"* (Matthew 27:46)

Prophecy: The Messiah will be given vinegar to drink: "*When I was thirsty they offered me vinegar.*" (Psalms 69:21)

This was fulfilled: "*There they offered Jesus wine mixed with a bitter substance.*" (Matthew 27:34)

 Prophecy: The Messiah would be buried with the rich: "*He was placed in a grave with the wicked, he was buried with the rich, even though he had never committed a crime or ever told a lie.*" (Isaiah 53:9)

This was fulfilled: "*When it was evening, a rich man from Arimathea arrived; his name was Joseph, and he also was a disciple of Jesus.......he asked for the body of Jesus.........Pilate gave orders for the body to be given to Joseph......so Joseph took it, wrapped it in a new linen sheet and placed it in his own tomb, which he had just recently dug out of solid rock.*"   (Matthew 27:57-60)

Prophecy: The Messiah's bones would not be broken: "*Not one of their bones is broken.*" (Psalms 34:20)

This was fulfilled: "*But when they came to Jesus they saw that he was already dead, so they did not break his legs........this was done to make the scriptures come true: 'Not one of his bones will be broken.'*" (John 19:33-36)

Prophecy: The Messiah will be pierced: "*They will look at the one whom they stabbed to death....*" (Zechariah 12:10)

This was fulfilled: "And there is another scripture that says, '*People will look at him whom they pierced'.*" (John 19:37)

These are just some examples of the numerous prophecies mentioned in the Old Testament writings and their fulfillment in the canonical Gospels. Other prophecies foretold John the Baptist would be the messenger for Jesus, the fore-runner who would prepare the way for him; the Messiah would be from the line of Abraham; the Messiah would be the descendant of Isaac; the Messiah would be a descendant of Jacob; the Messiah would be of the tribe of Judah; the Messiah would spend a season in Egypt; the Messiah would be born in Bethlehem; the Messiah would be heir to David's throne; the Messiah would speak in parables; the Messiah would be crucified with criminals; the Messiah would bring light to Galilee; the Messiah would heal the broken-hearted. All of these prophecies were written nearly 1,000 years before Jesus was born, and all of them were seen to come true in the canonical gospels!

And Jesus clearly knew about them!

In fact, Jesus knew he had to fulfil them!

'Do not think that I have come to do away with the Law of Moses and the teachings of the prophets. I have not come to do away with them, but to make their teachings come true.' (Matthew 5:17-18)

"Then Jesus began to teach his disciples. 'The Son of Man must suffer much and be rejected by the elders, the chief priests, and the teachers of the Law. He will be put to death, but three days later he will rise to life'. He made this very clear to them." (Mark 8:31-33)

"Once again Jesus took the disciples aside and spoke of the things that were going to happen to him. 'Listen,' he told them, 'we are going up to Jerusalem where the Son of Man will be handed over to the chief priests and the teachers of the Law. They will condemn him to death, and then hand him over to the Gentiles, who will mock him, spit on him, whip him, and kill him, but three days later, he will rise again.' " (Mark 10: 33-34)

So Jesus was clearly foretelling his own suffering on the cross and death.

But how did he know all this?

Simply because he knew the scriptures and the prophecies!

It was all there! Written down! Written down several centuries before Jesus was born!

All there in Psalm 22, written about 1,000 years before Jesus was born!

"My God, my God, why have you abandoned me?" (Psalm 22:1)

"But I am no longer a human being; / I am a worm, / despised and scorned by everyone! / All who see me jeer at me; / they stick out their tongues and / shake their heads. / 'You relied on the Lord,' they say, / 'Why doesn't he save you? / If the Lord likes you, / why doesn't he help you?" (Psalm 22:6-8)

"An evil gang is around me; / like a pack of dogs they close in on me; / they tear at my hands and feet. / All my bones can be seen. / My enemies look at me and stare./ They gamble for my clothes / and divide them among themselves." (Psalm 22:16-18)

So is it not perfectly clear? Jesus was simply fulfilling the prophecies! Herein lies the plot for the drama of the life of the person known to us as Jesus! His life mission? To fulfil the prophecies!

Everything, absolutely everything that happened in Jesus' life was geared towards fulfilling those prophecies! He repeatedly said so himself!

And why did he perform miracles? Again, Jesus answered this

question himself!

When John asked, from prison, if Jesus was the expected messiah, or should they look for another (Matthew 11:13), Jesus told his disciples to inform John of what he had done:

"The blind see, the lame walk, those who have leprosy are cured, the deaf hear, the dead are raised, and the good news is preached to the poor." (Matthew 11:5)

With these words, Jesus was declaring that his miracles were the fulfilment of the promises made in the ancient prophecies about the Messiah:

"When that day comes, the deaf will be able to hear a book being read aloud, and the blind, who have been living in darkness, will open their eyes and see". (Isaiah 29:18)

And:

"He has chosen me and sent me to bring good news to the poor, to heal the broken-hearted......" (Isaiah 61: 1)

So, if Jesus was simply fulfilling the prophecies, then he must have been very sure that he himself was the promised messiah.

But what made him different from all the other would-be messiahs we have seen who roamed the Galilee region at the same time?

Why did he himself think he was the messiah? Why was he so certain?

The answer lies in the Essene Brotherhood.

It is time for us to pay a visit to the Essenes! Time for us to hear what they have to say!

CHAPTER 9

THE PLAYERS: THE ESSENES

Jesus was not a lone operator, a one-man band, working alone and independently. Far from it! He was surrounded by a vast network of support in the form of energy workers, and a vast energy system, all put in place several centuries before he was even born.

In my previous books, I have explained all about energy, how it works and how we are always surrounded by subtle energy fields, linking all of creation, linking all planets and worlds in the entire cosmos, linking our microcosm that is earth, through the ley lines of the planet, with the macrocosmic entirety of the vast matrix of creation. The only difference between us here on Planet Earth and all the other countless planets, stars, worlds and civilisations that make up entire creation is a difference in energy vibration. And we are all One in the entirety of creation, in the infinity of creation, in the infinity of a greater Universal Intelligence that controls all things.

Yes, we plan our own lives. Yes, we determine what happens in our lives by the thoughts and words that we constantly send out in the form of subtle energy, into that vast universal energy network matrix. Energy attracts like energy. What we send out in energy, we get back. That's just the way it works!

The universe is like a mirror, reflecting our own image. When you look in the mirror with a scowl on your face, what do you see? A scowling face looking back at you, of course! What else can you possibly expect to see? And how do you get the scowling face in the mirror to change to a smiling face? By changing the mirror or the glass? Hardly! The only possible way to get that scowling face in the mirror to change to a smiling face in that same mirror is to change the expression on your own face! Then the reflection changes! Changes from the scowl to a smile! Change yourself, change the image in the mirror, and the universe responds likewise. That's just the way it is!

So yes, we are in control in that we attract everything to us from the same energy vibrational level as we send out.

But! As just mentioned, there is a Great Universal Intelligence over-seeing the entire grand plan, a Great Universal Intelligence in control of all things. And there is indeed a grand plan, a grand design, a grand master plan put in place to raise the Spiritual consciousness of humanity, to enable us all to return to our divine source. And within that plan, we all continue to operate with our free will. We can go off track, we can lose our way, we can drift into Spiritual exile, a Spiritual desert, a Spiritual wilderness, as we indeed constantly do! It is always our choice! We have free will!

Skeptics abound in every age. Today, we have those who will argue that if there is a Spirit world, or if there is life after death, then why has no one come back to tell us?

And the answer?

Does the butterfly return to being a caterpillar? Does the dragonfly return to being a grub?

We are not alone! We are never alone! There is no divide between us and the Spirit worlds, from where help and support are constantly being offered to us! Great, highly evolved beings from the upper echelons of the Spirit world have from time to time reincarnated here on this dense vibration energy frequency level of Planet Earth to walk amongst us and try and steer us back on track. But we have free will! We cannot be forced to do anything! These Enlightened beings can only show us, tell us. That's all they can do! The rest is up to us! We can take it or leave it! We have free will!

One of these Enlightened beings, one of these highly evolved entities, one of these high vibrational energy life forms was Yeshua ben Joseph, Yeshua son of Joseph, known to us as Jesus.

Yeshua reincarnated in Jewish Palestine 2,000 years ago when the spiral of Spiritual energy that had begun its downward movement after the fall of Atlantis had sunk so low on Planet Earth that it was in danger of getting stuck at the lowest level. So then a set of synchronicities was put in motion to offer mankind an opportunity to progress toward soul awareness, towards Ascension. There is no such thing as chance or coincidence. Everything that happens to us during our life-time and everyone we meet during our life-time is there for a purpose. We leave nothing to chance, for there is no such thing. All is synchronised in the great cosmic dance, the great cosmic tapestry, woven with the lives of each and every one of us, inter-twined, criss-crossing, inter-connected.

What was set in motion 2,000 years ago is coming together now at this particular point in time, synchronistic findings of long hidden material, together with new Spiritual techniques and understandings, all given impetus by the 2012 planetary alignment, the ending of several cosmic and planetary cycles, raising the earth's vibration to a level never experienced by humanity before, a level that enables more of the higher celestial energies to come through to us. The veil between the higher energy vibrational frequencies of the Spirit world and our dense earth vibration is thinning now very rapidly indeed. The time is fast approaching when many more will walk in both worlds jointly. A lot already do.

Yeshua was surrounded in his life by others, those who had specially volunteered at a soul level, to assist him in his life-mission.

His parents, for example, known to us as Mary and Joseph, both very highly evolved souls. In just the same way as we get to choose our parents, the parents who would be most suitable to help us fulfil our specific life-plan, so too with Jesus. And of course, his twin soul, Mary Magdalene!

And just like us, Jesus was subject to the laws of Planet Earth. Just like us, he had the veil pulled down over his eyes at birth. He did not arrive here with all the knowledge and wisdom he needed in order to fulfil his mission already within himself. Just like us, he too had to start to learn all over again.

He had to learn, he had to be taught.

And he was surrounded by those who were to be his teachers.

The Essenes! That ancient term of the sect of Judaism!

The Essene communities were a vital link, a vital part of the vast energy supply net-work that was to surround and support Yeshua. Yeshua was to teach the masses the difference between the reality of creation where the natural laws govern the entire cosmos, and the superstition that had derived from myths down through the centuries and instilled into people's minds in order to keep wealth and power in the hands of the few. Not an easy task! Not for the faint-hearted! Only the bravest of souls would ever take on the power and might of the Roman Empire and their fawning puppets, the religious and political authorities in Jewish Palestine, - the Sanhedrin, the Pharisees, the Sadducees, and the hated priests of the Temple.

Yes! The Essenes are the key to our understanding of Jesus' mission and to finding the real Jesus. '*The Way*' was the revolutionary way of life taught by Jesus, and the Essenes were known as '*Followers of the Way*'. Jesus himself said: '*I am the Way, the Light and the Truth*'.

And the reason why Jesus reincarnated in Jewish Palestine 2,000 years ago was because it was in Jewish Palestine 2,000 years ago that the Essene community were in existence! Jesus freely chose to reincarnate in a Jewish family who were part of the Essene community! They were essential to him in order for him to fulfil his life's mission! His life's mission to spread the truth about the nature of God, and humanity, the Oneness of all beings and the natural laws governing the entire cosmos.

The secretive, mysterious Essenes, who lived during the last two or three centuries B.C.E. and the first century C.E. were part of a vast extensive network system of Brotherhood extending through many centuries and many lands. They followed the teachings of ancient Persia, Egypt, India, Tibet, China and many other countries, transmitting all the knowledge in its most pure form. That esoteric knowledge was recorded in the Dead Sea Scrolls, found in caves in 1945 near the Dead Sea, where the Essene community of Qumran lived. In Palestine and Syria the members of the Brotherhood were called Essenes, with branches known as Nazoreans and Ebionites, and in Egypt as Therapeutae, or healers.

Their simple, pure, mainly agricultural, communal way of life, living on the shores of lakes and rivers, away from cities and towns, and sharing equally in everything, meant that there were no poor or rich amongst them. They established their own economic system, based entirely on the Law, and were living proof that all man's food and material needs can be attained without struggle, through knowledge of the Law. They were proficient in prophecy, healing, astronomy, all passed down from the Ancient Mystery Schools of Persia and Egypt. They sent out teachers and healers from their communities to teach the inner, esoteric knowledge to those outside the Brotherhood, to those who were ready to listen.

And two of those who were sent out from the Essene community at Qumran to teach and heal were John the Baptist and of course, Yeshua! Known as Jesus to us, known as Yeshua to the Essenes!

Not long after the canonical gospels and the Acts of the Apostles were written, around 80 C. E., the Essenes were no longer in existence. Their teachings and doctrines had become heresy, their texts and writings being destroyed just like all the other texts and writings that did not agree with the teachings of the early church fathers. Those early Roman church fathers who were not in the least interested in Yeshua the man, but in Jesus the god-man, created to compete with all the other Roman gods of the day, all born of virgins, all dying and resurrecting.

To understand the Essenes we must understand energy and how it works. We must understand that the energy ley-lines of the earth connect us to the other subtle energy fields surrounding us, in just the same way as our own Spiritual chakra system connects us to the Spiritual energies, or the energy meridian lines in our own bodies.

It is along these earth ley-lines that the energy is strongest, hence Spiritual apparitions or manifestations, when they do occur, occur along these ley-lines. So too with UFOs! It is also along these earth ley-lines that religious structures, burial grounds, old monuments, stone circles, Stonehenge, Newgrange, monoliths, even our own fairy rings here in Ireland, are all found, all in a straight line with each other, all following the ley-lines. All ancient cultures, during different time frames, knew full well about the existence and importance of ley-lines, and the connection of our Planet Earth with cosmic geometry. So too did the early Christian Church fathers! It can be no coincidence, because again, there is no such thing, that all church buildings are built over what the Christian church itself regarded as '*pagan*' sites! Even, or indeed, especially, the Vatican! Built over the Temple of Mithras, an ancient God to whom the Roman armies paid homage! Where these ancient Spiritual sites were established, that's where the energy was! That's why they were all established where they were! The shamans, the Native American Indians, the Spiritual indigenous cultures throughout history all knew what they were doing! And the Christian churches took the sites all over from them, castigating these same highly Spiritual peoples as pagans and setting out on their path of destroying them!

I asked you before, earlier in this book, can you name one country, just one country, that has ever benefitted from the coming of Christianity?

History clearly shows that the powerful Christian countries were only interested in increasing their power through the grasping of colonies and their material wealth. And what did they bring to these lands which they conquered? Only disease and disharmony! And where there had been a Spiritual way of life in total harmony with Mother Nature, in total Oneness with All That Is, this was replaced by so-called Christianity, wielding the double-edged sword of fear and guilt!

So yes, the earth has energy chakras, all connected up by energy lines, ley-lines, just as the human body has seven chakras, our own Spiritual energy points, all connected within each of us by our meridian energy lines, and connecting each and every one of us to the entire cosmic energy matrix. The energy lines of the earth, the ley-lines, run around the entire earth, and at certain points at equi-distance around the earth, they form energy vortexes. These are the earth's chakras. Glastonbury, in England is the heart chakra of the world. Other chakras include for example, Ayers Rock in Australia, centre of the Spiritual Aboriginal culture; Mount Shasta in California and Peru in South America. Looked at on a map of the world, when joined up through following the ley-lines, they form the shape of the dragon. And again, it can be no coincidence that these energy lines are known as Dragon lines in China!

And if we look at the earth's energy lines in Israel and Palestine, we find the fifth Chakra of the earth, the throat chakra, the communication chakra, right over the Mount of Olives!

And there were three distinct triangular settlements of Essenes communities around Jerusalem, itself built on an energy ley-line.

No coincidence! There is no such thing! Here we have the Essene communities, in three distinct places, along energy lines, in a triangular shape, reflecting cosmic geometry, all placed around Jerusalem. Sending energy along those ley-lines to Yeshua especially when he was on the cross!

So now that we have established the importance and significance of the Essenes in the life and times of Jesus, let us delve further and take a closer look!

The Essenes as an ancient Jewish sect are not mentioned in any of the canonical gospels or in any of the other writings in the New Testament. They are not mentioned any more than Mary

Magdalene is mentioned in her connection to Jesus.

No surprise there than!

And why are they not mentioned?

Maybe because they were so secretive and mysterious? Certainly every member of the Order was required to take a sacred oath at their initiation to never disclose any of the secrets of the Order to any person who did not belong to their community, and not to disclose to anyone else that he himself was a member.

But we have early historians and writers who do tell us about this secretive, mysterious Jewish sect. Obviously, those early church fathers were not interested in Yeshua the man, only Jesus the god-man!

Yes, the Essenes certainly did exist! But they were known under different names!

The first-century historian Flavius Josephus, Pliny, Dio Chrysostom and Hippolytus of Rome all spoke of this secretive and mysterious community of the Essenes. Dio Chrysostom, the Greek orator and philosopher also mentioned the Essene Community near the Dead Sea. His report is dated later than Pliny. While Josephus speaks of them as Essenes, mostly in Qumran, Philo of Alexandria speaks of them as the Theraputae, who are known to have been a branch of the Nazaraean Essenes. Many others refer to them as the Ebionites. Yet others simply as the Nazarenes. So the Nazarenes of the gospels are actually the Essenes. Jesus the Nazarene! Jesus the Essene!

"And so what the prophets said came true, 'He will be called a Nazarene' " (Matthew 4: 22-23)

And we saw earlier how Publius Lentulus, when describing Jesus to Tiberius Caesar, the Roman Emperor, wrote that Jesus' hair was *'parted in the middle of his forehead, after the manner of the Nazarenes'.*

BUT! This was NOT because he was from NAZARETH! Again, the gospels have misrepresented this information to us. Some scholars even claim that Nazareth as a place did not yet exist at the time of Jesus. If that is the case, and certainly Josephus does not mention Nazareth, then obviously the gospel writers have created a mythical Nazareth for Jesus their mythical god-man!

At Paul's trial as related in Acts, the high priest Ananias and those who made their charges against Paul concluded:

"We have, in fact, found this man a pestilent fellow, an agitator among all the Jews throughout the world, and a ringleader of the sect of Nazarenes". (Acts 24:5)

So Paul appears to have been a Nazarene, an Essene!

Hippolytus of Rome, writing two centuries later, gave a lengthy account of the Essenes, very similar to that of Josephus, but with some new material, though Hippolytus himself of course, was not an actual eye-witness to the Essenes.

But again, it is from Flavius Josephus, the famous Jewish historian and priest-general at the time of the Jewish war, also contemporary with the Essenes who gives us the earliest description. Josephus lived both before and after the destruction of Jerusalem by Titus in 70 C.E. and he tells us he himself belonged to the Essene order for a while, and had undergone the required term of probationship or trial for three years:

"When I had reached my sixteenth year did I undertake to examine

into our different religious sects and their doctrines, that having come to know them I might choose the one that appeared the best.................Having resolved this, did I at once begin to prepare myself in different ways that I might be found worthy to be admitted into the Order of Essenes. In order to accomplish this, I turned to a man called Banus, of whom was told that he belonged to the Brotherhood of Essenes, and lived in the wilderness, made his clothes out of the bark and leaves of the trees, fed upon wild fruits, plants and herbs, and from holiness bathed several times night and day in cold water...........In this man's company I spent three entire years, undergoing all kinds of trials, temptations and privations, and then returned to the city (Jerusalem). When I had filled my nineteenth year did I commence to shape my life and habits according to the doctrines of the Pharisees........"

The nineteen year old Josephus, however, soon tired of the Essenes and their rigid, frugal, life-style and tried the life of the Pharisees, which he found to be much more to his taste. But the fact that he was inside the Essene Community for those initial three years certainly qualifies him to talk about them. His accounts are contained in his works *'Jewish Antiquities'* and *'The Jewish War'*, written between 70 and 100 C.E.

So what does Josephus say about the Essenes?

"The Essenes are despisers of riches, and so very communal as to earn our admiration. There is no one to be found among them who has more than another; for they have a law that those who come to join them must let whatever they have be common to the whole order, so that among them all there is no appearance of either poverty or excessive wealth. Everyone's possessions are intermingled with every other's possessions; as if they were all brothers with a single patrimony...

They have no one city, but in every city dwell many of them; and if any of the sect arrive from elsewhere, all is made available to them as if it were their own; and they go to those they have never seen before as if long acquaintances. Thus they carry nothing at all with them in their journeys, except weapons for defense against thieves. Accordingly, in every city there is one appointed specifically to take care of strangers and to provide them with garments and other necessities.

In their clothing and deportment they resemble children in fear of their teachers. They change neither their garments nor their shoes until they are torn to pieces or worn out by time. They neither buy nor sell anything to one another, but each gives what he has to whomever needs it, and receives in exchange what he needs himself, and even if there is nothing given in return, they are allowed to take anything they want from whomever they please."
(Antiquities 18.2.5 18-22)

We have seen that the Essenes are not mentioned by name in the New Testament. However, the similarities shown in Josephus' account between their organisation and that of the disciples, for example holding possessions in common, simplicity of clothing, travelling from town to town carrying almost nothing and relying on finding welcome in a sympathetic house, has led scholars to theorise that Jesus no doubt had his origins in the Essenes:

"Don't take anything with you on your journey except a stick - no bread, no beggar's bag, no money in your pockets. Wear sandals, but don't carry an extra shirt.' He also said, "Wherever you are welcomed, stay in the same house until you leave that place".
(Mark 6:8-10)

"Do not carry any gold, silver or copper money in your pockets; do

not carry a beggar's bag for the journey or an extra shirt or shoes or a stick. Workers should be given what they need.......When you come to a town or village, go in and look for someone who is willing to welcome you, and stay with him until you leave that place". (Matthew 10:9-11)

"The group of believers was one in mind and heart. None of them said that any of their belongings were their own, but they all shared with one another everything they had. With great power the apostles gave witness to the resurrection of the Lord Jesus, and God poured rich blessings on them all. There was no one in the group who was in need. Those who owned fields or houses would sell them, bring the money received from the sale, and hand it over to the apostles, and the money was distributed to each one according to his needs. And so it was that Joseph, a Levite born in Cyprus, whom the apostles called Barnabas (which means 'One who Encourages)', sold a field he owned, brought the money, and handed it over to the apostles." (Acts: 4:32-37)

Furthermore, the description of John the Baptist preaching in the desert and baptising in the River Jordan also suggests a connection to the Essene community near the Dead Sea, as they too performed a ceremonial cleansing using water, either pouring water over themselves or immersing themselves totally in it.

It is from Josephus indeed, that we get the very first reference to the Essenes, when he writes about the death of Antigonus which happened in 103 B.C.E. Here Josephus relates how the Essenes had an uncanny ability to successfully predict future events, and how the death of Antigonus at the hands of his brother Aristobulus was accurately foretold by an Essene named Judas, who, according to Josephus, was *'an Essene born and bred.'* On this particular occasion, according to Josephus, Judas, a teacher of the Law, was sitting near the Jerusalem Temple teaching a number of his pupils:

"The sect of the Essenes maintain that Fate governs all things, and that nothing can befall man contrary to its determination and will.......... the Essenes are Jews by race, but are more closely united among themselves by mutual affection, and by their efforts to cultivate a particularly saintly life.......... they renounce pleasure as an evil, and regard continence and resistance to passions as a virtue.......they disdain marriage for themselves, being content to adopt the children of others at a tender age in order to instruct them.......despise riches..........when they enter the sect, they must surrender all of their money and possessions into the common fund, to be put at the disposal of everyone.........one single property for the whole group...... they regard oil as a defilement, and should any of them be involuntarily anointed, he wipes his body clean..............they make a point of having their skin dry and of always being clothed in white garments............they are not just in one town only, but in every town several of them form a colony........they carry nothing with them when they travel..........they are, however, armed against brigands........ they do not change their garments or shoes until they have completely worn out........they neither buy nor sell anything among themselves...... they give to each other freely and feel no need to repay anything in exchange.........before sunrise they recite certain ancestral prayers to the sun as though entreating it to rise. They work until before mid-day when they put on ritual loincloths and bathe for purification. Then they enter a communal hall, where no one else is allowed, and eat only one bowlful of food for each man, together with their loaves of bread.......they eat in silence..... afterwards they lay aside their sacred garment and go back to work until the evening.............at evening they partake dinner in the same manner..........during meals they are sober and quiet and

their silence seems a great mystery to people outside......... their food and drink are so measured out that they are satisfied but no more........... they see bodily pleasure as sinful..........on the whole they do nothing unless ordered by their superiors, but two things they are allowed to do on their own discretion: to help those 'worthy of help' and to offer food to the needy...... they are not allowed, however, to help members of their own families without permission from superiors............ they are very careful not to exhibit their anger, carefully controlling such outbursts.....they are very loyal and are peacemakers......they refuse to swear oaths, believing every word they speak to be stronger than an oath......... they are scrupulous students of the ancient literature...........they are ardent healers in the healing of diseases, of the roots offering protection, and of the properties of stones.............those desiring to enter the sect are not allowed immediate entrance. They are made to wait outside for a period of one year. During this time, each postulant is given a hatchet, a loincloth and a white garment. The hatchet is used for cleanliness in stooling for digging and covering up the hole. Having proved his constinence during the first year he draws closer to the way of life and participates in the purificatory baths at a higher degree, but he is not yet admitted into intimacy. His character is tested another two years and if he proves worthy he is received into the company permanently..........they are sworn to love truth and to pursue liars. They must never steal. They are not allowed to keep any secrets from other members of the sect; but they are warned to reveal nothing to outsiders, even under the pain of death................. those members convicted of grave faults are expelled from the order. In matters of judgement Essene leaders are very exact and impartial. Their decisions are irrevocable......... they are so scrupulous in matters pertaining to the Sabbath day that they refuse to go to stool on that day..............they always give way to the opinion of the majority, and they make it their duty to obey their elders............. they are divided into four lots according to the duration of their discipline, and the juniors are so inferior to their elders that if the latter touch them, they wash themselves as though they had been in contact with a stranger.......... they despise danger. They triumph over pain by the heroism of their convictions, and consider death, if it comes with glory, to be better than the preservation of life....... they died in great glory amidst terrible torture in the war against the Romans............. they believe that their souls are immortal, but that their bodies are corruptible...... they believe that the soul is trapped in the body and is freed with death......... some of the Essenes became expert in forecasting the future."

In his second account, Josephus tells us:

"The Essenes declare that souls are immortal and consider it necessary to struggle to obtain the reward of righteousness. They send offerings to the Temple, but offer no sacrifices since the purifications to which they are accustomed are different. For this reason, they refrain from entering into the common enclosure, but offer sacrifice among themselves. They are holy men and completely given up to agricultural labor."

Josephus' writings on the Essenes are supported and corroborated by other early writers. We have first hand reports of the Essenes from Philo of Alexandria, the Greek-speaking Jewish philosopher of the Egyptian Diaspora, who lived between 30 B.C.E. and 40 C.E. and was, therefore contemporary with Jesus. Philo writes about the so-called '*Therapeut*', a branch of the Essenes, the word '*Therapeut*' meaning a physician, and his description of the Essene Order corresponds with that of Josephus, giving us two separate, independent accounts of the doctrines, customs, life and rituals of

the Essene Brotherhood.   According to Philo, the 'Therapeuts' were
those members of the Essene Brotherhood who willingly chose to
retire into solitude and spent their time studying nature and in
meditation. They lived in several places in Egypt and Palestine,
with their largest community near Alexandria in Egypt. Some lived
in the desert and in caverns, amongst these being Banus, with
whom Josephus spent three years. And as we have seen, the
description we are given of John the Baptist in the canonical
gospels, of his way of life and his habits almost certainly confirms
that he too was one of these remote Therapeuta.

Philo's writings about the Essenes come down to us through two
works, 'Quod omnis vis probus liber sit' (Every truly upright man is
free) and 'Apologia pro Judais', the latter of which has been lost
but the information was retained by the early church father
Eusebius in his 'Praepaeatio Evangilica':

"They do not offer animal sacrifice, judging it more fitting to render
their minds truly holy. They flee the cities and live in villages where
clean air and clean social life abound. They work either in the fields
or in crafts that contribute to peace. They do not hoard silver and
gold and do not acquire great landholdings; procuring for
themselves only what is necessary for life. Thus they live without
goods and without property, not by misfortune, but out of
preference. They do not make armaments of any kind. They do not
keep slaves and detest slavery. They avoid wholesale and retail
commerce, believing that such activity excites one to cupidity. With
respect to philosophy, they dismiss logic, but have an extremely
high regard for virtue. They honour the Sabbath with great respect
over the other days of the week..............they believe God causes all
good but cannot be the cause of any evil...... they honor virtue by
foregoing all riches, glory and pleasure. Further, they are convinced

they must be modest, quiet, obedient to the rule, simple, frugal and without mirth. Their life style is communal. They have a common purse. Their salaries they deposit before them all, in the midst of them, to be put to the common employment of those who wish to make use of it. They do not neglect the sick on the pretext that they can produce nothing. With the common purse there is plenty from which to treat all illnesses. They lavish great respect on the elderly. With them they are very generous and surround them with a thousand attentions. They practise virtue like a gymnastic exercise, seeing the accomplishment of praiseworthy deeds as the means by which a man ensures absolute freedom for himself."

Philo further tells us:

"The Essenes live in a number of towns in Judea, and also in many villages and in large groups. They do not enlist by race, but by volunteers who have a zeal for righteousness and an ardent love of men. For this reason there are no young children among the Essenes. Not even adolescents or young men. Instead they are men of old or ripe years who have learned how to control their bodily passions. They possess nothing of their own, not house, field, slave nor flocks, nor anything which feeds and procures wealth. They live together in brotherhoods and eat in common together. Everything they do is for the common good of the group. They work at many different jobs and attack their work with amazing zeal and dedication, but in obvious exhilaration. Their exercise is their work. Indeed, they believe their own training is to be more agreeable to body and soul, and more lasting, than athletic games, since their exercises remain fitted to their age, even when the body no longer possesses its full strength. They are farmers and shepherds and beekeepers and craftsmen in diverse trades. They share the same way of life, the same table, even the same tastes: all of them loving

frugality and hating luxury as a plague for both body and soul. Not only do they share a common table, but common clothes as well. What belongs to one belongs to all. Available to all of them are thick coats for winter and inexpensive light tunics for summer. Seeing it as an obstacle to communal life, they have banned marriage."

Pliny the Elder, the Roman writer, who died in 79 C.E. reports about the Essenes in his work *'Natural History'*.

"To the west of the Dead Sea the Essenes have put the necessary distance between themselves and the salubrious shore. They are a people unique of its kind and admirable beyond all others in the whole world; without women and renouncing love entirely, without money and having for company only palm trees. Owing to the throng of newcomers, this people is daily reborn in equal number; indeed, those whom, wearied by the fluctuations of fortune, life leads to adopt their customs, stream in great numbers. Thus, unbelievable though this may seem, for thousands of centuries a people has existed which is eternal yet into which no one is born: so fruitful for them is the repentance which others feel for their past lives!"

Even the early church father Eusebius, as we have seen, wrote about the Essenes around 300 C.E:

"Even in our day, there are still those whose only guide is Deity; ones who live by the true reason of nature, not only themselves free but filling their neighbours with the spirit of freedom. They are not very numerous indeed, but that is not strange, for the highest nobility is ever rare; and then these ones have turned aside from the vulgar herd to devote themselves to a contemplation of nature's verities. They pray, if it were possible, that they may

reform our fallen lives; but if they cannot, owing to the tide of evils and wrongs which surge up in cities, they flee away, lest they too be swept off their feet by the force of the current. And we, if we had a true zeal for self-improvement, would have to track them to their places of retreat, and, halting as supplicants before them, would beseech them to come to us and tame our life grown too fierce and wild: preaching instead of war and slavery and untold ills, their Gospel of Peace and freedom, and all the fullness of other blessings."

So much for the ancient accounts of the Essenes, which all support and corroborate each other. But we have modern evidence as well! Very modern evidence in the form of new historical research! Synchronistic developments indeed!

Past-life regressions! Past-life regressions, where a person accesses memory recall into a former life! And what a valuable contribution to our research into the life and times of Jesus! Into the life of the Essene communities!

Dolores Cannon was a past-life regression therapist who, as part of her work, periodically met clients who had previously spent lives contemporary to Jesus. In her two best-selling books, *'Jesus and The Essenes'*, published in 1992 and *'They Walked With Jesus'*, published in 1995, she gives an account of the recorded details delivered by clients who were part of the Essene community at the time of Jesus. These particular clients knew absolutely nothing about the Essenes prior to regression, and indeed after the session, remembered nothing. All the accounts support each other, even though these people did not know each other and had never met before in this life-time. What they delivered, under regression, supports the accounts of the early writers. More proof, indeed, if ever we needed more, of the existence of the Essenes and their importance in the life of Jesus!

And not just Dolores Cannon! We also have the combined work of Stuart Wilson and Joanna Prentis, who have spent the last twenty years researching the Essene communities, the life of Jesus and the powerful teachings of Mary Magdalene. They too have been using past-life regression to unearth amazing and fascinating evidence to bolster up our understanding of the ancient Essene sect, of whom Jesus is now without doubt believed to have been a member. Wilson and Prentis together published their best-selling 'The Essenes: Children of the Light' in 2005, followed by 'Power of the Magdalene' in 2009 and 'The Magdalene Version' in 2012.

Putting all this together, as well as the Dead Sea Scrolls, believed to be the writings of the Essene community themselves at Qumran, we now have a remarkable amount of reliable historical evidence and information, much more so than ever before.

Much more so than ever before, simply because the Essenes were by nature, highly secretive and mysterious, so only a limited knowledge could be given to us from the early writers, as they had no access to the inner secrets, apart of course from Josephus, and even he could not disclose the inner secrets, not only because he was not yet party to them, but because vows of secrecy curtailed him from disclosing much.

But these modern day regressions afford us access, bring us right into the Essene communities themselves! We are getting the inside picture! We are given the secret insights into this mysterious, secretive community, and indeed into their core group, the select inner circle who knew most about Jesus, and whose special responsibility was to protect Jesus.

So what do we learn about the Essenes from these past-life

regressions?

One of Dolores Cannon's clients under regression was called Suddi, a teacher in the Essene community in Qumran, who taught none other than John the Baptist and Jesus himself! Through Suddi, we have inside information into the Essene community, their way of life, their healings, their teachings, and of course an insight into the life of Jesus himself.

But in order to understand how past-life regression works, we need to first understand and accept that we have all had numerous past and former lives, in all their diversity. We all tend to reincarnate in groups, in various aspects of our whole soul, with members of our own Monad, our soul family, time and time again. So too with Jesus. Jesus had already had many life times, some as female, others as male. He is known to have spent a previous life-time in Atlantis, for example, as a high priest of the Order of Melchizadek. By the time he reincarnated as Yeshua ben Joseph in first-century Jewish Palestine, he was already a highly advanced soul, returning to the dense earth plane from the highest of the Spiritual energy frequency levels.

Many of the souls here on earth today are also from the Essene community, voluntarily re-incarnating at this point in time to bring to light once again the teachings of Jesus, teachings which have been concealed, hidden and misrepresented for the last 2,000 years by those who sought to manipulate and control us for their own devious, mercenary ends. In their hands, Jesus has become merely a pawn, part of their power game, branded and exploited in the interests of self.

Yes, Jesus was an Essene. As were Anna, the grandmother of Jesus, Joseph and Mary the parents of Jesus, Joseph of Arimathea the wealthy uncle of Jesus and the sister of Jesus' mother Mary, Mary Magdalene and John the Baptist, all of whom together formed the nucleus of the surrounding support net-work set up to see Jesus fulfil his life-mission this time around. Coincidence? There is no such thing! Synchronicity? It all has to be! It can be nothing else!

So let us now return to the Essenes and what they were about.

Their lives were certainly, by all accounts, devoted entirely to achieving perfection and purity. They were definitely strongly connected to the Ancient Mystery Schools. As we have seen, the Nazoreans were a branch of the Essenes, and Jesus was a member of the Nazoreans. There were Nazorean villages on the slopes of Mount Carmel, hence many scholars now believe the name given to the village of Nazareth. Mount Carmel itself was a place spoken of with reverence by ancient Egyptian priests, a place where Pythagoras himself, the father of mathematics and philosophy, studied, the place of the Oracle and Altar of the prophet Elijah who later reincarnated as John the Baptist, and of course, the place where Jesus too was taught what he needed to know in order to be able to fulfil the prophecy of himself as the promised Messiah.

The Essenes were teachers and very advanced healers. Most of their teachings were communicated orally, as was the custom of that time, most people being unable to read or write.

And what did they teach?

Obviously, since they were strongly connected to the Ancient Mystery Schools and the Druids, they taught the ancient Mysteries, exactly what we read about in a previous chapter. One of the strengths of the Essenes was their ability to draw from and absorb key elements in other wisdom traditions, including Pythagorean concepts, Egyptian Mystery School material and Zoroastrianism.

And their prophecies were apocalyptic! They saw the world in a state of war between the Forces of Darkness and the Forces of Light, about to clash in a grand finale, with the end times approaching. Yeshua himself said:

"Remember that all these things will happen before the people now living have all died." (Matthew 24:32-35)

"I assure you that you will not finish your work in all the towns of Israel before the Son of Man comes." (Matthew 10:23)

"For the Son of Man is about to come in the glory of his Father with his angels, and then he will reward each one according to his deeds. I assure you that there are some here who will not die until they have seen the Son of Man come as King." (Matthew 16:27-28)

Yes! Jesus was an Essene! Certainly his teachings were Essene teachings!

Their secret greeting, *"Peace be with you"* was repeated constantly by Jesus throughout the canonical gospels. And when Judas betrayed Jesus:

"Judas went straight to Jesus and said, 'Peace be with you, Teacher', and kissed him."

So Judas too must obviously have been an Essene!

Jesus was baptised by John in the River Jordan, baptism being a sacred institution and an initiation long practised by the Essenes. As were the breaking of bread and the passing of the wine.

A further central theme in their teaching and which occurs frequently in their texts was the idea of God as both Father and Mother, both male and female. This, of course, would have been anathema to the Jewish authorities surrounding Jesus, steeped as they were in the traditions and superstitions of a male god, and in a patriarchal society, and they would have regarded Jesus as a dangerous radical who was undermining their Judaic traditions.

The gospel of the Essenes tells us:

"Seek not the law in thy scriptures, for the law is Life, / Whereas the scriptures are only words./ I tell thee truly/ Moses received not his laws from God in writing,/ But through the living word. / The law is living word of living God / To living prophets for living men./In everything that is life is the law written./ It is found in the grass, in the trees,/ In the river, in the mountains, in the birds of heaven, / In the forest creatures, and the fishes of the sea; / But it is found chiefly in thyselves. / All living things are nearer to God / Than the scriptures which are without life. / God so made life and all living things / That they might by the everliving word / Teach the laws of the Heavenly Father / And the Earthly Mother / To the sons of men./ God wrote not the laws in the pages of books,/ But in thy heart and thy spirit. / They are in thy breath, thy blood, thy bone; / In thy flesh, thine eyes, thine ears, / And in every little part of thy body. / They are present in the air, in the water, / In the earth, in the plants, in the sunbeams, / In the depths and in the heights. / they all speak to thee / That thou mayest understand the tongue and the will / Of the living God. / The scriptures are the works of man, / But life and all its hosts are the work of God." (Translated from the original Hebrew and Aramaic texts of the Gospel of the Essenes, by Edmond Bordeaux Szekely)

This is exactly what Jesus was teaching, and this is exactly what got him into so much trouble with the Pharisees, the Sadducees and the Jewish authorities. Jesus was telling them that God is not found in the scriptures or in temples or synagogues but in every aspect of Nature and inside oneself.

Josephus has given us some words of the Essene Master Banus, with whom he spent three frugal years in an isolated location:

"Your Father is the Cosmos. Your Mother is Nature. Your siblings are your fellow humans. Live in harmony with the laws and forces of the Universe, Nature and of your own being. Preserve thyself. Learn the natural and cosmic laws. Live in peace with yourself, with humanity, with Nature and the Universe. Live in creative love with and for your fellow humans that they may live for thee. Peace Be With You."

There again, is the Essene signature greeting, their secret password, the secret sign by which they recognised one another, *'peace be with you!'*

"For my part, I carry all my wealth within me." (From Original Hebrew and Aramaic Texts Translated and edited by Edmond Bordeaux Szekely)

Again, exactly what Jesus was teaching!

Jesus came into conflict with all sections of Jewish society, steeped as they were in superstition, idolatry and offering of blood sacrifices to appease an angry god. The Pharisees regarded the scriptures literally, failing to understand the spiritual meaning of the coming of the promised Messiah. The Pharisees are known as the sect of egotism and hypocrisy, and Jesus often castigated them as such. They observed all the outward forms of the Mosaic Law, but their holiness was merely for outward show. Their haughtiness, greed and ambition negated any genuine form of real purity of heart or true humanity. Jesus several times warned against these false teachers, urging the people to shun their false doctrines:

*"How terrible for you, teachers of the Law and Pharisees! You
hypocrites! .... Blind guides!..........Blind fools!........... You snakes
and children of snakes!"* (Matthew 23: 13- 27)

Obviously no love lost there!

The Sadducees fared no better with Jesus than did the Pharisees.
The Sadducees denied the life of the soul and therefore also a life
after death. They interpreted the commandments as being a guide
to life, and if adhered to, then one would have an easier passage
through life. They were of wealthy stock, and generally considered
the wealthiest amongst the Jews. Herod himself belonged to the
sect of the Sadducees and acknowledged their doctrines. They
controlled the goings on at the Temple, luxuriating in the
splendour and ceremony that was part of the daily life there.

It is therefore very clear how the third Jewish sect, the Essenes,
differed totally from the other two main sects in Jewish society,
the Pharisees and the Sadducees. And it is very clear why and how
Yeshua, as an Essene teacher, made enemies in all places.

However, although Jesus openly criticised and castigated the
Pharisees, the Sadducees and the Priests of the Temple at every
opportunity he got, he never once spoke against the Essenes!

Suddi, in Dolores Cannon's book, 'Jesus and the Essenes, tells us
that the Essenes regarded themselves as *"a school of thought, not
a religion"* and confirms for us how the Jewish people felt towards
the Essenes:

S: *"They are greatly feared by those who are in power, because we
have studied into the mysteries that others have only hinted at.
And they fear that if we gain too much power and knowledge that
they will lose their place."* ('Jesus and the Essenes' Chapter 3,

Page 24)

Likewise Jesus' attitude toward women. Jesus had many women amongst his disciples, all accompanying him on his mission and supporting him financially:

"Mary Magdalene.........Joanna, whose husband Chuza was an officer in Herod's court; and Susanna and many other women who used their own resources to help Jesus and his disciples." (Luke 8:1-3)

And Suddi again supports this:

S: "In most synagogues women are not even allowed inside. They have the women's terrace...........
S: "It is said that one away from the other is not complete. So all knowledge must be shared, so that it can never be lost. I have known women who have more brains than the average rabbi." (Jesus and the Essenes, Chapter 3, Page 25)

And again:

... "In the synagogues the women are not allowed except in the women's court. Here all are allowed." ('Jesus and the Essenes' Chapter 5, Page 41)

And we know Mary Magdalene was well learned in spices and herbs and in ointments and oils for healing, from the Egyptian Schools, and from her training in the Temple of Isis. And it was Mary Magdalene, of course, who anointed Jesus with the very expensive oil, the sacred significance of which the other male disciples completely failed to understand.

Suddi also tells us about Jesus' disciples:

S: "There are both men and women followers, although there are

*at times slightly more women than men, because the female
develops better. They are more receptive to things of this nature
than the male.......*
*S: "And he wanted to protect the women from those who did not
understand. And so the disciples were sent out in pairs. Usually
they were paired up according to their charts."* ('Jesus and the
Essenes, Chapter 24, Page 253)

So Jesus' disciples were a balance of male and female, reflecting
the balance of Father-Mother God. The gospels tell us that Jesus
sent out 72 more disciples, but leads us to believe that they were
all male. The gospels also keep from us the fact that many of Jesus'
original 12 disciples had their wives travelling with them!

The Essenes were very advanced healers, healing on many levels,
using herbs, oils, ointments, crystals and clay, all as in the Ancient
Mystery Schools. Jesus himself, as we shall see in the next chapter,
as a healer often used clay mixed with spittle.

Evidence of Essene healings is seen again in both Dolores Cannon's
books '*Jesus and the Essenes*' and '*They Walked With Jesus*' and
also in '*Essenes: Children of the Light*' by Wilson and Prentis,
where, under regression, several clients reported that the Essenes
used sound and crystals in their healings as well as oils, ointments,
herbs, spices and clay.

The Essenes healed on many levels. They believed and worked on
the premises that if the physical body was suffering from an illness
or sickness, then it was out of tune, out of balance with the overall
harmony of the universe and entire creation. That meant an
imbalance of energy. So the Essenes were channelling energy from
higher vibrational levels into the soul of the person with the illness,
in order to restore the balance, to return the person to a state of

harmony, a state of wellness once again. The Essenes could operate on a multi-dimensional level, communicating with the soul in order to determine how to apply the required healing, *for the greatest good of the person.*

And why was that a strict stipulation, *for the greatest good of the person?*

Simply because the soul of the person, at a deeper level, has already chosen what that person needs to endure or experience in the physical body in order to evolve spiritually. Removing that illness, sickness or disability might not always therefore, be for the greatest good of that person. We all have lessons to learn in each life-time, and if we fail to learn them in one life-time, those lessons will present themselves in front of us time and time again in future life-times until we do indeed learn them. That's the way it all works! We have to learn our lessons!

The Essenes, especially the higher level ones, and hence Jesus, could read all of this in the aura, the spiritual magnetic energy field surrounding each and every one of us, and which reflects not only our physical condition, but also our inner soul state and our spiritual level of development. Jesus could see how far on that person was in learning that particular lesson with which the illness was associated, and he could tune in to the soul of that person to determine if healing was or was not appropriate at this point in time. But not even Jesus could interfere with the life-plan of any particular soul, and so not everyone who came to Jesus was physically healed.

Modern day Reiki and holistic practitioners operate in the same way, always stipulating, *for the highest good* of the client. And always seeing the person in front of them as a perfect being, holding that vision before them, and invoking the higher celestial energies to flow down and link with the physical body. The practitioner is not the healer and must always remember that. They are only the channel, the conduit, the door-opener, allowing the higher vibrational energy to enter and flow to where it is needed.

The Essenes were highly advanced healers, simply because their pure way of life enabled them to clear away any obstacles or barriers within themselves, therefore enabling them to connect strongly with the pure energy of the cosmos, and to be a perfect channel through which the healing energy could flow.

We are all healers, yes!

But we cannot operate from our base consciousness level. Healing and channelling of higher vibrational energy requires a raising of our own consciousness, a shift to a higher state of consciousness. This higher state of consciousness is what Reiki and holistic practitioners are taught how to achieve, through various meditation techniques and through being attuned to various sacred symbols which activate and strengthen the healing power within each of us.

The Essenes were expert at all of this. And they learned it all from the ancient Mystery Schools and the Druids. And Jesus learned it from the Essenes! The Essenes were the teachers of Jesus, preparing him to fulfil the prophecy:

"The blind will be able to see and the deaf will hear. The lame will leap and dance, and those who cannot speak will shout for joy." (Isaiah 35:5-6)

Jesus was a Jewish rabbi, a teacher and healer, who had purposely incarnated into *a* Jewish family who were involved with the Essenes. Some scholars believe he became their *'Teacher of Righteousness'* meaning *'Teacher of the right use of energy'* about whom we learn in the Dead Sea Scrolls.

The Essenes were a Jewish sect representing an esoteric, an inner, a spiritual aspect of Judaic Judaism. They were mystics, their totally pure way of life enabling them to access higher vibrational levels of spiritual energy far above the norm. They taught and practised astrology, prophecy, soul travel and psychic development.

And it was their skills in astrology and astronomy that enabled them to determine when and how the birth of Jesus would come about!

Jesus' parents, Joseph and Mary both belonged to the Essene community, as did his maternal grandmother Anna.

The prophecies had said:

"The Lord says, 'The time is coming when I will choose as king a righteous descendant of David. That king will rule wisely and do what is right and just throughout the land. When he is king, the people of Judah will be safe, and the people of Israel will live in peace. He will be called 'The Lord Our Salvation'. " (Jeremiah 23: 5-6)

The Essenes arranged the marriages of their members according to their birth charts, matching them to create the perfect union. Suddi in *'Jesus and the Essenes'* tells us:

S: "She was chosen by the elders to be instructed and for her destiny to be made known to her. It was known from her birth whom she would be. And her parents were of us." (Chapter 22, Page 230)

And when asked, under regression by Dolores Cannon, D: *"Did they choose her from others?"*, Suddi replied:

S: *"How can we choose the mother of the Messiah? It is not up to us. That is up to Yahweh* (the Jewish name for their God). *But he allowed us to know, so that we might instruct her and perhaps guide her upon the path. The elders knew but they did not choose. It is said that there are others whose charts could possibly have fit, but there was study and it was decided that.......this was the only basic decision that I can think of was made. The chart was read and it was finally understood in what it meant............*
S: *"It is said that it has to do with the points at which the stars lie when you are born, and the path that you take while you live....*
S: *"The only thing as far as someone's decision, is about the interpretation of these charts. There were several girls who were born at approximately the same times that it was possible. And therefore, the ultimate interpretation came about. This was when it was discovered that she would be the mother of the Messiah."*
('Jesus and the Essenes', Chapter 22, Page 230 - 231)

Of course, the Essenes knew the prophecies about the birth of the expected Messiah! They knew all the prophecies! And of course they knew the genealogies involved and what was required to fulfil those prophecies!

There was to be no virgin birth!

In the Gospel of Philip, found at Nag Hammadi in 1945 and not numbered amongst the canonical gospels, we read:

"Some say that Mary was impregnated by the grace of the Holy Spirit, but they do not know what they say. How can the Feminine impregnate the feminine?"

No matter what the canonical gospels might claim! No matter what story the early church fathers might endorse for their own personal gains! No matter what was to trundle on down through history as one of the foundation stones of the Christian church and one of their basic doctrines!

There would be no virgin birth!

No! This was to be a marriage arranged by two members of the Essene community, two who between them would meet the genealogical requirements specifically and essentially stipulated in the prophecies!

This was to be a marriage which would produce the expected Messiah!

And such a pair were of course, Joseph and Mary! Both Essenes! Both trained and learned in the Essene ways!

And yes! It was the Essenes who determined all that!

They knew the prophecies. They knew all about the promised Messiah. And their main purpose, their main function, their main reason for existence was to bring about the prophecy and see it through to the very end. They were the ones who interpreted the birth charts! They were the ones who facilitated the whole procedure!

Hence their mysterious disappearance again shortly after the Crucifixion of Jesus!

They had fulfilled their mission!

The Crucifixion marked the end of their supporting Jesus, their Teacher of Righteousness. They had seen him through the task which was his destiny. The Crucifixion signalled the end of the whole development of the Essene communities, and it signalled the end of the highly spiritual Essene way of life.

Yes, the Essenes spawned, birthed, raised and fitted Jesus for his role as the Messiah for the Jewish people!

They were the tailors who cut the cloth exactly according to the design! Jesus was tailor-made to order! Tailor-made in order to fulfil the ancient prophecies!

Again, Suddi confirms for us:

S: ... "Their pathway (that of John the Baptist and Jesus) has been determined by the teachers. The elders know. They have knowledge of this, but it is for their path." ('Jesus and the Essenes' Chapter 21, Page 225)

The Essenes protected Yeshua in his young life until he was old enough to be initiated into the secret Order as a member, with his cousin John. Yeshua, after becoming a member, knew all the secrets and duties of the Brotherhood. Yet he did not join one or other of their particular solitary communities. Jesus knew his mission was to travel and preach to the people, fully aware at the same time that he was putting his own life in danger. And when his life was in danger, the secretive Essene Brotherhood could not save him because their laws forbade them to interfere in public or political matters.

And another of the Essene teachings was that the highest reward, the greatest glory for any Essene was to die for the truth and faith! And Jesus had this firmly fixed in his mind as he travelled around the Galilee area, preaching and teaching the truth to the crowds and endangering his own life in the process. Jesus willingly suffered death in order that he might draw attention to the great truths of nature and its elements, rather than the superstitious beliefs instilled into the Jewish people.

At what particular and exact stage in his life Jesus learned of his destiny is of course, impossible to ascertain, but he certainly knew of it by the beginning of his ministry when he was 30 years of age, as he constantly referred to himself as the Messiah and fulfilling the prophecies!

And he certainly knew that those prophecies included his own Crucifixion!

We saw in the first chapter of this book *WHY* Jesus was *CRUCIFIED*. Not just killed, but *CRUCIFIED.*

It is now time for us to take a closer look at that crucifixion of Jesus, and to ask a further, vital question.

What question do we now need to ask?

We need to ask *DID JESUS REALLY DIE ON THE CROSS?*

But before we consider this, we need to look at Jesus the healer and exorcist, because in order to fulfil the prophecies, which was Jesus' mission, Jesus had to be able to heal:

 "............the deaf will be able to hear a book being read aloud, and the blind, who have been living in darkness, will open their eyes and see". (Isaiah 29:18)

"He has chosen me and sent me to bring good news to the poor, to heal the broken-hearted......" (Isaiah 61: 1)

CHAPTER 10

JESUS: TEACHER, HEALER AND EXORCIST

We live in a world where science dominates our lives. If we cannot experience something with our five physical senses, then we tend to disbelieve, to discredit, even to scoff and ridicule, dismissing it all as fantasy, misguided logic, our over-active imagination. Hence, we tend to see medical science as providing the answer to all ills, aches and pains.

But since time began, and before science took over in this world in which we live, people have had access to healings and cures, and what we would now call miraculous happenings, although perfectly natural to them.

Use of natural herbs and plants, witch-doctors, witches, spells, cures, charms, astrology, shamans, - all have played their part in changing societal thinking and belief systems down through the centuries. Indigenous peoples have always had their own natural methods of healing.

And it was no different in first-century Jewish Palestine.

They too had their beliefs about disease and sickness, what caused them and how they could be cured. In the context of first century Jewish Palestine, sickness and illness were understood to be the divine punishment for sin, and the priests of the Temple were the only ones qualified by the Torah to diagnose and administer to the afflicted. Sin was believed to be brought by the devil, in the on-going battle between the forces of good and the forces of evil. Mental illness necessitated the expulsion of the inhabiting evil spirit, linked, in the mind, with this particular affliction. So sickness of any sort, sin and the devil were three inter-connected, inter-dependent and inter-related realities. Sickness was the punishment for sin, brought about by the devil. Subsequently, healing or recovery from sickness or illness meant forgiveness from God for sin.

While we have seen that the canonical gospels are not reliable as historical evidence, they do nevertheless present us with some perfectly credible information concerning the work of Jesus as a healer. When all the distortions, all the contradictions, all the inaccuracies, all the fabrications are considered and when all the bias has been accounted for, there is still a wealth of material left in the remaining residue for us to sift through.

We can see too, from the Dead Sea Scrolls and from the historian Josephus and others that healings beyond the ordinary understanding of man were being performed contemporary to Jesus.

Multiple cures are described throughout ancient writings, attested to and verified by those who witnessed such happenings. The Dead Sea Scrolls attest to the Essene Communities who, as we have just seen, were exceptionally gifted, seasoned and well-practised healers.

Just like such places as Lourdes or Fatima today, where numerous people have claimed to be cured, and where crutches are left as testimony to those who walked away without needing them anymore. We have seen earlier how these place are all connected to the energy ley-lines of the earth, where cosmic energy is strongest.

Of course there are sceptics. There have been sceptics in every age!

Even in Jesus' time!

"When his family heard about it, they set out to take charge of him, because people were saying, 'He's gone mad!' " (Mark 3:20-21)

Others believed differently:

"Some teachers of the Law who had come from Jerusalem were saying, 'He has Beelzebub in him! It is the chief of the demons who gives him the power to drive them out.' " (Mark 3:22)

To understand these healings and what appeared to be miraculous cures, we need to enter the world of energy, the world beyond our dense human planetary vibrational level. Today, healings are taking place beyond human understanding and normal abilities. Shamans and Reiki and Holistic practitioners across the world have brought to us the proof that healings are occurring beyond the human level. Indeed, in one of my previous books, *'A World of Healing'* you can read in the final chapter titled 'Michelle's Story', about a healing which defied the doctor's explanation, a healing which I myself witnessed.

So what was Jesus actually doing?

Jesus was moving energy around! Jesus was moving spiritual healing energy through his own body! What he was taught to do by the Essenes and in the Ancient Mystery Schools!

The change in the sick person's condition sometimes came about by simply touching the garment of Jesus, and on one occasion Jesus enquires who it was, as he felt the energy go out from him:

"There was a woman who had suffered terribly from severe bleeding for twelve years, even though she had been treated by

many doctors. She had spent all her money, but instead of getting better she got worse all the time. She had heard about Jesus, so she came in the crowd behind him, saying to herself, 'If I just touch his clothes, I will get well.'

*She touched his cloak, and the bleeding stopped at once; and she had the feeling inside herself that she was healed of her trouble. **At once Jesus knew that power had gone out of him**, so he turned round in the crowd and asked, 'Who touched my clothes?'*

His disciples answered, 'You see how people are crowding you; why do you ask who touched you?'

But Jesus kept looking round to see who had done it. The woman realized what had happened to her, so she came, trembling with fear, knelt at his feet, and told him the whole truth. Jesus said to her, 'My daughter, your faith has made you well. Go in peace, and be healed of your trouble.' " (Mark 5:25-34)

"He had healed many people, and all those who were ill kept pushing their way to him in order to touch him." (Mark 3:10)

"And everywhere Jesus went, to villages, towns, or farms, people would take those who were ill to the market places and beg him to let them at least touch the edge of his cloak; and all who touched it were made well." (Mark 6:56)

Strong claims indeed, by any standard!

But did they really happen?

Indeed, when we move forward in time to the Middle Ages, we find in the writings of Shakespeare references to this same belief that there were certain holy people around who were gifted with the power of healing, and all one needed to do was touch the hem of their garment as they passed by. King Edward the Confessor of England was believed to have had the cure of scrofula, '*the king's evil*', a disease in which the glands swelled and broke out through the skin. Edward's successors to the throne inherited the power, and James I was one of those successors. He kept up the ceremony of touching the sufferers, although he himself thought that any subsequent relief came from the patient's faith rather than from any miracle.

Speaking about King Edward the Confessor. we learn from the Doctor in Shakespeare's 'Macbeth':

"There are a crew of wretched souls / That stay his cure. Their malady convinces / The great assay of art; but at his touch / Such sanctity hath heaven given his hand, / They presently amend."
('Macbeth': Act 4, Scene 3, lines 141-144)

And Malcolm replies:

"A most miraculous work in this great king, / Which often, since my here-remain in England, / I have seen him do. How he solicits heaven, / Himself best knows; but strangely-visited people, / All swollen and ulcerous, pitiful to the eye, / The mere despair of surgery, he cures, / Hanging a golden stamp about their necks, / Put on with holy prayers; and 'tis spoken, / To the succeeding royalty he leaves / the healing benediction. With this strange virtue / He hath a heavenly gift of prophecy, / And sundry blessings hang about his throne / That speak him full of grace." ('Macbeth': Act 4, Scene 3, lines 148-158)

Even today, we too have our beliefs in certain unorthodox methods of healing! We have unexplainable cures and charms for such ailments as ringworm, shingles, sprains, migraines, colic, to name but a few, many of these cures being handed down from father to son, generation after generation.

So now let us take a closer look at other healings with which Jesus has been credited.

And not just at WHAT he did, but also at HOW he did it!

Several times in the synoptic gospels and in the gospel of John, we read how Jesus was practising popular medicine of the age. For example, human spittle was believed to have curing, therapeutic powers, and was especially beneficial in curing eye diseases.

Well, we cannot argue with that! A cat, dog, or any other animal today will, literally, lick its wounds. We have all witnessed that! So too, we tend to suck our thumbs, or apply mouth suction or our tongue to a sore or a sting. A baby constantly sucks its thumb, as indeed do even older people!

And, of course, DNA tests are done using spittle. So there must, literally, be something in it! Something that heals, something that administers comfort or relief, something that tells a lot about us! And those wise people who understand and communicate with plants will confirm that when introducing a new plant into your house or garden, a little of your own spittle around the roots will create a strong bond between you and your plant, by instilling some of your DNA into it.

Let us now return to Jesus and his use of spittle!

"They came to Bethsaida, where some people brought a blind man to Jesus and begged him to touch him. Jesus took the blind man by the hand and led him out of the village. After spitting on the man's eyes, Jesus placed his hands on him and asked him, 'Can you see anything?'

The man looked up and said, 'Yes, I can see people, but they look like trees walking about.'

Jesus again placed his hands on the man's eyes. This time the man looked intently, his eyesight returned, and he saw everything clearly." (Mark 8:22-25)

And again:

"As Jesus was walking along, he saw a man who had been born blind. His disciples asked him, 'Teacher, whose sin caused him to be born blind? Was it his own or his parents' sin?'

Jesus answered, 'His blindness was nothing to do with his sins or his parents' sins. He is blind so that God's power might be seen at work in him.'

After he said this, Jesus spat on the ground and made some mud with the spittle; he rubbed the mud on the man's eyes and said, 'Go and wash your face in the pool of Siloam'. So the man went, washed his face and came back seeing." (John 9:1-7)

Here we see Jesus refuting the prevalent belief that sin caused illness and disease. And we saw in the previous chapter that the Essenes used clay in their healings. Here Jesus is doing the same thing.

On another occasion, Jesus cured a man's deafness with the same method of using his spittle:

"Some people brought him a man who was deaf and could hardly speak, and they begged Jesus to place his hands on him. So Jesus took him off alone, away from the crowd, put his fingers in the man's ears, spat, and touched the man's tongue. Then Jesus looked up to heaven, gave a deep groan, and said to the man,

'Ephphatha', which means, 'Open up!'

At once the man was able to hear, his speech impediment was removed, and he began to talk without any trouble." (Mark 7: 32-35)

On other occasions, Jesus took the afflicted person by the hand, for example, when Peter's mother-in-law was ill with a fever:

"He went to her, took her by the hand, and helped her up. The fever left her, and she began to wait on them." (Mark 1: 31)

Luke, however, tells us:

"He went and stood by her bedside and ordered the fever to leave her. The fever left her, and she got up at once and began to wait on them." (Luke 4:39)

So on occasions, he simply commanded the illness to leave, more often in the case of exorcising evil spirits:

"Jesus ordered the spirit, 'Be quiet and come out of the man!' The demon threw the man down in front of them and went out of him without doing him any harm." (Luke 4:35)

"Demons also went out from many people, screaming, 'You are the Son of God!'

Jesus gave the demons an order and would not let them speak, because they knew that he was the messiah." (Luke 4:41)

At other times, he placed his hands on the person:

"One Sabbath Jesus was teaching in the synagogue. A woman there had an evil spirit that had made her ill for eighteen years: she was bent over and could not straighten up at all. When Jesus saw her he called out to her, 'Woman, you are free from your illness!'

He placed his hands on her, and at once she straightened herself up and praised God." (Luke 13: 10-13)

"A man suffering from a dreaded skin disease came to Jesus, knelt down, and begged him for help. 'If you want to,' he said, 'you can make me clean.'

Jesus was filled with pity, and stretched out his hand and touched him. 'I do want to,' he answered. 'Be clean!' At once the disease left the man, and he was clean." (Mark 1:40-42)

The gospels also report Jesus raising people from the dead for example, Jairius' young daughter:

"Jesus went into the room where the child was lying. He took her by the hand and said to her, 'Talitha, koum', which means, 'Little girl, I tell you to get up!'

She got up at once and started walking around. She was only twelve years old." (Mark 5:41)

Jesus is even reported as healing from a distance, for example:

"When Jesus entered Capernaum, a Roman officer met him and begged for help: 'Sir, my servant is sick in bed at home, unable to move and suffering terribly.'

'I will go and make him well,' Jesus said.

'Oh no, sir,' answered the officer. 'I do not deserve to have you come into my house. Just give the order, and my servant will get well.............

Then Jesus said to the officer, 'Go home, and what you believe will be done for you.'

And the officer's servant was healed that very moment." (Matthew

8:5-13)

So, what are we to make of all this?

Did Jesus or did Jesus not perform these cures?

Remember! The gospels were written to glorify Jesus and build him into a miracle-working marvel! So of course there is going to be a lot of hyped-up over-exaggeration!

But even after we take this into account and allow for it, there can be no doubt that Jesus was indeed healing people. That can be no surprise to us, as we know he learned healing techniques from the Essene Community, who were very advanced healers. And he learned in the Mystery Schools! And we have seen how the Essenes were an integral part of the plan to bring the Messiah to earth, and how they fitted him out to perform what was required of him in that particular role. The prophecies had to be seen to be fulfilled! And the prophecies, as we saw earlier, foretold that the Messiah would perform healings and cures!

"Jesus went all over Galilee, teaching in the synagogue, preaching the Good News about the Kingdom, and healing people who had all kinds of disease and sickness. The news about him spread through the whole country of Syria, so that people brought to him all those who were suffering from all kinds of diseases and disorders: people with demons, and epileptics, and paralytics - and Jesus healed them all. Large crowds followed him from Galilee and the Ten Towns, from Jerusalem, Judea, and the land on the other side of the Jordan." (Matthew 4:23-25)

We read in the canonical gospels, those four gospels especially selected by the early church fathers, about how Jesus administered healing, and by spiritual means, to great numbers of people.

Is it therefore not very strange and somewhat contradictory, to say the least, that while the canonical gospels devote so much time to Jesus healing people, Christian churches today, and the Catholic Church in particular, refuse to acknowledge, and in fact condemn such spiritual healing practices?

Jesus' ability to heal was, for the early Christian church fathers, clear proof that Jesus was divine. His healings were considered miracles, which only someone of divine nature could possibly do. And a time limit was put on them! They ended when Jesus' life ended. Healings like what Jesus did were relegated to the early Church. And to the early Church only!

But! In my previous book, 'Are Ye Not Gods?' we saw that the pivotal core teaching of Jesus was that we are ALL of divine nature, there is divinity in all of us. And because of that, as Jesus said:

"I say unto you, he that believeth in me, the works that I do he shall do also; and greater works than these shall he do." (John 14:12)

"In my name they will drive out demons.......they will place their hands on sick people and they will get well." (Mark 16:18)

But all this spiritual healing was, according to church teaching, for Jesus only and could not be performed by any human being, because, according to church teaching, Jesus was divine and no other human being is divine. But, we can all heal! We all have that inherent ability!

And in order to protect the divinity of Jesus, the early church fathers developed the teaching that sickness and illness are part of God's will for us. By suffering pain, they rationalised, we are getting closer to God, atoning for our sins and accepting the will of God. Suffering is necessary for us to get close to God! Healing of any kind transgresses God's will! Suffering is the way to heaven!

Where did all this come from? Where in the gospels does Jesus teach us this? Those same gospels which the Church claims are the basis of Church teaching?

The early Church taught that suffering was a necessary part of life. The Roman Emperor Justinian closed down the medical schools of Alexandria and Athens in 529 C.E., and in 1215 C.E. Pope Innocent III condemned surgery. Then in 1248, dissection of the body was pronounced sacrilegious and the study of anatomy was condemned. In fact, if we look at the history of the development of medicine and surgery down through the ages, we can clearly see that it was the Catholic Church that was the chief obstacle to any progress. The body was the temple of God and could not be desecrated by surgery, whether alive or dead. It was only when medieval medical men began to dissect dead human bodies that anatomy was able to become a scientific study, leading to all the modern findings in the field of medicine. Close observation was the key to finding out what the human body really looked like, and it was the great artists, painters and sculptors of the medieval Renaissance who portrayed and exposed the human body as it is, for the first time, allowing medical science to progress. We have all heard about the body snatchers, those who stole bodies from graveyards in order to experiment on them. This body snatching was a direct result of the church ban on investigation of any kind into the human body. Now, today, a person can willingly donate his body to medical science!

So, according to the church teaching, was Jesus then in his healings transgressing natural law?

"Do not think that I have come to do away with the Law of Moses

*and the teachings of the prophets. I have not come to do away with
them, but to make their teachings come true."* (Matthew 5:17)

Jesus was not a magician!

He was simply operating within the natural laws!

Just as today where thousands of holistic practitioners, shamans
and those who channel healing spiritual energy through Reiki and
other spiritual channels are operating within the natural laws!

And what do we mean by operating within the natural laws?

It's all about energy again!

Everything, absolutely everything is energy in some form or other.
And energy never dies. It just changes form.

As any holistic, shamanic or Reiki practitioner will tell you, when
the physical body manifests illness or sickness, that illness, sickness
or dis-ease has originated in one of the other bodies surrounding
the physical body,- the emotional body or the spiritual body, for
example. The actual dis-ease itself only manifests in the physical
body, it is not caused by the physical body. It is always emotionally
or mentally induced, so the cure must require mental or
emotional adjustment and not physical treatment. Remember, we
are not just a body! We are spiritual beings! So to cure or heal the
dis-ease, the cause of the dis-ease needs to be found. The cause is
never physical, always emotional, mental or spiritual, working its
way inwards to manifest in the physical body. Energy flows
constantly throughout the whole body, in tandem with the energy
that flows throughout the entire cosmos. Any illness is trapped
energy, and needs to be released. The body needs to be made
whole again, the physical, mental, emotional and spiritual put back
in balance. Spiritual healing administers a healing that balances the

whole body, brings it back into harmony with itself and back into harmony with the great universal energy. Imbalance is an unnatural thing. Balance is a natural position. Man is naturally healthy and that health comes from within, it is not imposed by external forces.

The shamanic worldview is that we are all one; one with each other; one with the cosmos and one with the realm of Spirit. And so we are all inter-connected, inter-dependent, not just with each other, but with the whole environment and the entire vast network of energetic transactions that is constant and on-going. Healing is the balancing of all these energies, in tandem, within the person. Healing is connecting with one's own soul, our own very essence, where one finds that great reservoir of infinite universal energy that we call God.

Healing requires a shift in consciousness. In fact healing *is* a shift in consciousness. No healer can administer healing unless he first raises his own consciousness above the base consciousness level where, unfortunately, most people spend most of their time. Healing is seeing wholeness in the wholeness of entirety in the flowing energy of the entire creation. Illness is the result of disharmony within the being of the sick person himself.

And it is the whole body that the holistic and Reiki practitioner sees. The perfect, whole and complete spiritual body, the inner divine light. There is divine light within each and every one of us, no matter how deep in the darkness we appear to be. When you look in the mirror, what do you see? Most often, you see just your body. That's your body *just in* the mirror. But when you look *through* the mirror, you see a very different image! You see the spiritual you, the total person you are in spirit. This is the image the spiritual healing therapist holds when administering healing energy. This is you, perfect in your God energy. This is you, a perfect expression of the divinity of God and of your own divinity. This part of you never gets sick. It cannot. It is perfect in every way. This is the wholeness of you that transcends any physical suffering or pain. This does not mean a denial of pain, for such a claim is beyond reason. But they are only part of the whole picture. You are NOT your pain or your illness. You must see yourself as already whole! That is how the Reiki or holistic practitioner sees you!

Spiritual healers do not work in opposition to the medical profession, but rather in tandem with it, each complementing the other. Of course there are times when medical surgery is necessary and vital. But we must always ask ourselves, what brought this illness on in the first place? What is my body trying to tell me here?

Again, it's all about energy, energy flow and keeping the energy flowing, the energy within the physical body in balance with the other emotional, mental, spiritual energy bodies that surround the physical body in the aura, and the energies that are flowing throughout the universe and within the entire cosmos. We are all connected! What affects one, affects all!

And furthermore, as any subtle energy healer will tell you, the two essential energy streams, known as the 'masculine' and the 'feminine' must also be in balance in each and every one of us. We are currently suffering from an imbalance in these two energies, the scales tipped very much in favour of the masculine. Our present excess of masculine energy in the world has created a warring, violent world, where competition is rife, success comes at any price, where only the fittest survive, and where a person is judged by the amount of material possessions and money he has managed to accrue.

Jesus and Mary Magdalene chose to come here to Planet Earth in Jewish Palestine 2,000 years ago when the masculine energy was also very much to the fore, Jewish society being male-dominated, patriarchal and even misogynistic. But Jesus and Mary Magdalene did not just re-incarnate for the Jewish people. No one particular culture or race can claim a monopoly on their teachings. Their lives and teachings do, yes, reflect the times and place in which they lived as physical beings, but those same teachings transcend space and time, resonating with all cultures, all times and all places.

Everything must be in balance. Everything must be in harmony. Harmony within the physical body reflecting the harmony of all the cosmic energies. And when disharmony occurs, illness follows in its entourage.

Yeshua of course knew all this. He could read in people's auras where the problem was, and administer the required healing energy. He could tap into a person's soul and see if healing was appropriate at that particular time, or if healing would in any way negate the plan of the soul. Jesus did not heal everyone who came to him, as even Jesus could not interfere with another person's life or soul plan.

So why, one might ask, can we not do the same thing?

Of course we can! Jesus told us we can!

"I say unto you, he that believeth in me, the works that I do he shall do also; and greater works than these shall he do." (John 14:12)

Jesus did not originate spiritual healing or create the spiritual healing law. He simply practised it! But he was the Master-Healer!

Shamans, Reiki and holistic practitioners all operate within this natural law of flowing universal energy.

The spiritual healing law simply states that man is essentially, first and foremost, a spiritual being. The spiritual healing law places emphasis on the wholeness of each person, all energies in balance. It is when these energies are out of balance that illness occurs, and therefore the cure can only happen when these energies are re-aligned.

And how does one activate one's own healing power?

We are all healers, each one of us with the power to heal. This power can only be activated when our consciousness is sufficiently raised, through meditation, spiritual growth or an increased spiritual awareness.

Man has an inherent right to be healthy. Jesus said: *'It is not the will of your Father who is in heaven that one of these little ones should perish.'* (Matthew 18:14)

God does not punish through ill health.

Jesus, at the pool at Bethzatha, near the Sheep Gate in Jerusalem asked the man who had been ill for 38 years:

'Do you want to get well?' (John 5:6)

What a daft question, one might say!

But! Some people cling to sickness, for various reasons, and do not really want to get well! Sad but true! Illness guarantees many people yearned-for attention and sympathy! One can even indulge in self-pity through the illness, or even escapism. That cold is too comfortable with you to go away! You are nurturing it, molly-coddling it! And then of course, there is sickness benefit! How many people cling to illness rather than go back to work, because they are better off being ill? And some people are not happy unless they are miserable, with something to complain about, usually health issues. Yes, these people are all taking comfort and security in some way from being ill! And of course, that is a catch-22 situation! They send out the thought that they are ill, and that is mirrored in the universal energy field, and returned in like! What you send out you get back! You create your own reality!

Are you willing to take command of the forces within you and issue an executive order? The force of will is essential! If you desire healing with all your heart, if you accept it and are willing to let go of everything less than wholeness in mind or body, then you most certainly can and will be healed. God does not heal! You heal yourself from within! It's all about claiming your own wholeness! Perceiving yourself as whole, complete and perfect!

We must remember, however, that any particular disease or illness may very well be part of our own life plan! And we cannot interfere with that plan! Even Jesus could not heal everyone who came to him, because he could see that particular person's soul and could see if that illness was there for a spiritual reason.

It is now time to return to answer the question : *DID JESUS REALLY DIE ON THE CROSS?*

Eileen McCourt

CONCLUSION: Did Jesus really die on the cross?

We began this book with the Crucifixion of Jesus, asking why was Jesus not just killed, but C*rucified*? Now we have come full circle, and we find ourselves back at the crucifixion scene once again, this time with a different question, this time with the pivotal question around which this book has been written.

DID JESUS REALLY DIE ON THE CROSS?

This question requires either a *yes* or a *no* answer. It cannot be both. Either he did or he did not. So which is it?

First, let us look again at some particular words in the ancient prophecies, those ancient prophecies which we have clearly seen played such an important part in the life of Jesus:

"But he endured the suffering that should have been ours, the pain that we should have borne. All the while we thought that his suffering was punishment sent by God. But because of our sins he was wounded, beaten because of the evil we did. We are healed by the punishment he suffered, made whole by the blows he received.

All of us were like sheep that were lost, each of us going his own way. But the Lord made the punishment fall on him, the punishment all of us deserved.

He was treated harshly, but endured it humbly; he never said a word. Like a lamb about to be sheared, he never said a word..............

The Lord says, 'It was my will that he should suffer; his death was a sacrifice to bring forgiveness' ....

He will know that he did not suffer in vain. My devoted servant, with whom I am pleased, will bear the punishment of many and for

175

his sake I will forgive them........ He willingly gave his life and shared the fate of evil men. He took the place of many sinners and prayed that they might be forgiven." (Isaiah 53:4-12)

The Book of Isaiah is named after a great prophet who lived in Jerusalem in the latter half of the eighth century B.C.E. The book may be divided into three principal parts, and this chapter 53 comes from a time when many of the people of Judah were in exile in Babylon, crushed and without hope. The prophet proclaimed that God would set his people free and take them home to Jerusalem, to begin a new life. They needed reassurance that God was going to fulfil his promise to them.

Let us now take another look at the Nicene Creed:

'I believe in one God / the Father, the Almighty, / creator of heaven and earth, / of all that is seen and unseen. / I believe in one Lord, Jesus Christ, / the only Son of God, / eternally begotten of the Father. / Through him all things were made. / For us men and for our salvation / he came down from heaven: / by the power of the Holy Spirit / he became incarnate of the Virgin Mary, and was made man. / For our sake he was crucified under Pontius Pilate; / he suffered death and was buried. / On the third day he rose again / in accordance with the Scriptures; / he ascended into heaven / and is seated at the right hand of the Father. / He will come again in glory to judge the living and the dead, / and his kingdom will have no end. / We believe in the Holy Spirit, the Lord, the giver of Life, / who proceeds from the Father and the Son. / Together with the Father and the Son he is worshipped and glorified. / He has spoken through the Prophets. / We believe in one holy catholic and apostolic Church. / We acknowledge one baptism for the forgiveness of sins./ We look for the resurrection of the dead, / and the life of the world to come. Amen.'

We can clearly see a direct link here between Isaiah's prophecy and the early church Nicene Creed. Both clearly state that Jesus died for our sins, and by his death on the cross, mankind was redeemed.

This is the belief on which the Roman Christian Church is founded.

But what if Jesus did not actually die on the cross?

There are many who would say that it is irrelevant whether Jesus died on the cross or not. Surely it is all symbolic anyway? Is his death on the cross not symbolic for Jesus showing us that death will be transcended by each and every one of us? Is the message not that we will all survive death?

On the other hand, there are millions who think that to find the correct answer is of the utmost importance. Is not the entire Christian Church teaching and declared ethos built around and centered on the actual death and resurrection of Jesus? Iconic images of the death of Jesus are everywhere. Every year, in the days coming up to Easter, elaborate rituals and ceremonies draw believers into churches across the world to celebrate these mysteries around which the church has maintained its authority and power for over 2,000 years.

But I have shown in previous books that the gospels are not reliable historical records. They are theological writings, written, changed, manipulated, distorted, interpolated, in order to establish the new Roman religion, that religion that competed with all other Roman and Greek beliefs in various gods who were all born of virgins, all died and resurrected again to save mankind.

We have seen earlier that Jesus' mission was to fulfil the ancient prophecies that a Messiah would come to earth and save mankind from spiritual decay. And Jesus' miracles made the people believe that he had the divinely given power necessary to overthrow the oppressors of Israel and to restore the kingdom of David. But we must remember that Jesus was dealing with a Jewish people steeped in the tradition of superstition and bigotry! A people tied in spiritual bondage, open to believing any sign of the supernatural or divine! So obviously, when word of Jesus having resurrected from the dead began to spread, there were only too many people willing to latch on to it and truly believe that their god had manifested all this for them. And the same with the earth quake that reportedly occurred as Jesus died on the cross. A people given to superstition are always prone to bursts of excitement and hysteria when they hear of what they consider to be supernatural happenings, miracles, delivered by the hand of God. Such people, in such an aroused state of excitement, tend to see what they want to see, what they need to see when something mysterious happens. An earth quake is a natural phenomenon, a clearing out, a release of energy from the bowels of the earth. But those who were there at the Crucifixion of Jesus saw all this as a sign from the heavens that Jesus truly was the Son of God!

This is 2017. Up until the middle of the twentieth century, the only evidence we had to go on was what was written in the New Testament, and even that we were not encouraged to read for ourselves.

However, as we have seen, a lot more information has come to our attention since then in a synchronistic series of findings, which makes those of us who are ready to listen, and ready to hear, question the whole teachings of the Christian Church surrounding the death and resurrection of the Jesus of the New Testament.

And what has Josephus to say on the matter? Josephus tells us about the reports of the resurrection. And he treats them as just reports, not facts:

"But for my part I know not which speak more correctly (those who say the body of Christ was stolen away or those who say that he rose from the dead). *But others said that it was not possible to steal him away, because they set watchmen around his tomb, 30 Romans and 1000 Jews."*

This large Jewish presence and the small Roman one are certainly not reported in the canonical gospels! Moreover, if this information from Josephus were to be true, then there is no possibility that Jesus' body could have been stolen away.

It would be logical to assume that crucifixion always meant certain death. How could anyone endure that horrendous torture and yet remain alive? But, we have evidence from Josephus to the contrary:

"And when I was sent by Titus Caesar with Cerealins, and a thousand horsemen, to a certain village called Thecoa, in order to know whether it were a place fit for a camp, as I came back, I saw many captives crucified, and remembered three of them as my former acquaintance. I was very sorry at this in my mind, and went with tears in my eyes to Titus, and told him of them; so he immediately commanded them to be taken down, and to have the greatest care taken of them, in order to their recovery; yet two of them died under the physician's hands, while the third recovered."

Victims of crucifixion were left on the cross for days on end, as a warning and a deterrent, eventually eaten by scavenging birds, or, if they were taken down, the remains were thrown into a communal burial pit. Death, when it did come, was from asphyxiation after the legs of the victim were broken at the knee, rendering him unable to breathe.

However, if they were taken down from the cross after a relatively short period of time, a few hours perhaps, and before their legs were broken, then they could just perhaps survive.

Jesus was taken down from the cross after a relatively short period of time. And his legs were not broken!

So what do I believe?

I can take the politician's favourite route and avoid answering this question altogether, spinning it around to some other slant. Or I can point out the sequence of considerations that would lead one to a certain conclusion.

First of all, I need to specify very clearly that I do not intend that my reply should be forced on any reader. I am not claiming infallibility. The pope has the monopoly on that one! Nor am I going to persecute, torture or declare war on any and all who differ from me. The Church has the monopoly on that! I can only explain, which I am perfectly willing to do, the process of thinking that has led me to my particular conclusion.

- The first key to understanding the life and mission of Jesus lies, as we saw, in the Ancient Mystery Schools and the Ancient Mystery Teachings. These existed thousands of years before the time of Jesus, the sacred knowledge being passed down orally to specially selected students. We saw how Jesus was most certainly a student at some of these schools, the esoteric knowledge that he gained being part of his own teachings in his ministry. But that esoteric content of his teachings has been kept from us. We have just been given the parables, as Jesus gave to the people who were not on a high enough spiritual consciousness level to understand the inner meanings.

- The second key to understanding the life and mission of Jesus lies, as we also saw, in the prophecies of the Old Testament. Jesus certainly knew these, as he told his disciples many times, and as the canonical gospels tell us many times, everything that was said and done was in order to fulfil the prophecies. And one of those prophecies was that he would be crucified!

- And the third and final key to understanding the life and mission of Jesus lies in the Essene community, established in various pivotal positions throughout Palestine and Galilee from 300 years before Jesus was born. Jesus was referred to in the gospels as *'Jesus the Nazarene'*. This, as we saw earlier in the chapter on the Essenes, does not mean Jesus from Nazareth. Many scholars claim that Nazareth did not even exist at the time of Jesus and that it was a false name created for the false god-man of the gospels. The Nazarenes were, like the Ebionites, a branch of the Essenes. Hence we are talking about Jesus as a member of the community of the Essenes.

- The Essenes were a secretive and mysterious people, deeply embedded in the ancient Mystery Schools, teaching the knowledge of those ancient mysteries to their specially chosen and selected students, passing everything down orally so the precious knowledge would not fall into the hands of the wrong people. They were above the common superstitions and bigotry of their time, being well informed in the natural laws of the universe and the secrets of nature. What has been shrouded in mystery and the supernatural in the gospels was natural and rational to the Essenes. Their writings were hidden deeply in caves, to escape detection and destruction, after the final destruction of Jerusalem by Titus in 70 C.E. and the dispersion of the remaining followers of Jesus.

- When the Dead Sea Scrolls, the writings of the Essene Brotherhood were discovered in 1947, they immediately became the greatest threat to orthodox Christian churches because they disclosed, for the first time, the teachings and way of life of these Essene communities, who called themselves 'Followers of the Way'. And Jesus himself said: 'I am the Truth, the Way and the Light'. Jesus was 'The Way' and they were 'Followers of the Way'. Their leader was 'The Teacher of Righteousness', meaning the teacher of the right use of energy.

- I have already explained in this book, and in a previous book, how what we now know about these Essenes has changed our whole understanding of the life and mission of Jesus. Clearly, early Christianity had its origins in the Essenes, and the Essenes were in fact the first Christians. But this has been kept covered by orthodox Christian churches. They were a secret Brotherhood, with their secret greetings and passwords, sworn to secrecy on all matters concerning the Brotherhood, and dispersed throughout Palestine and on the borders with Egypt, supporting and protecting Yeshua throughout his ministry.

- The Essenes were a mysterious people, linking the ancient Mysteries to the time of the life of Yeshua. They appeared very mysteriously and they disappeared just as mysteriously shortly after the Crucifixion of Yeshua.

- We know from Dolores Cannon's books and Wilson and Prentis' 'The Essenes, Children of the Light' on past-life regression, where various subjects, under deep hypnosis freely disclosed information about which they knew absolutely nothing when in their normal every-day state of consciousness, and had no recollection even of what they had disclosed when they were returned to that state of consciousness after the regression session ended. It is from these books that we get so much inside information about the Essenes and their secret ways and teachings.

- We learn directly from the mouths of these ancient Essenes through these past-life regression sessions that their mission in life was to send out teachers to teach *'The Way'*, to fulfil the ancient prophecies and establish the conditions on earth that would facilitate the coming of a Saviour, a Messiah, who would establish once again God's kingdom on earth.

- Yeshua was to be that Messiah, Yeshua ben Joseph, Yeshua son of Joseph. This Yeshua was to be fostered by the Essene community and taught the deep mystyeries of the ancient Mystery Schools in order to equip him to fulfil his mission as prophecied by the Old Testament. Jesus is the name given to him by the gospels, the Romanised version of Yeshua. But he was not known as Jesus in his own life-time. He was Jeshua, Yeshua ben Joseph. It was during the council of Nicea in 325 C.E., convened by the Emperor Constantine to bring some sort of unity and cohesion to his new Christian church that the name of Jesus was confirmed, all other names declared heresy.

- Jesus, throughout the canonical Gospels, several times says that he is fulfilling a prophecy of the Old Testament. For example, in Luke's Gospel, after his Resurrection, he told his disciples: *"These are the very things I told you about while I was still with you: everything written about me in the Law of Moses, the writings of the prophets, and the Psalms had to come true...........This is what was written: 'The Messiah must suffer and must rise from death three days later, and in his name the message about repentance and the forgiveness of sins must be preached to all nations, beginning in Jerusalem'."* (Luke: 24:44-47)

- The prophecies said that the Messiah would be of the House of David: *"The Lord says: The time is coming when I will choose as king a righteous descendant of David.'"* (Jeremiah 23: 5) The Essenes were knowledgeable in the prophecies. They were adept at reading the stars and interpreting life-charts. They matched Mary and Joseph according to their birth charts and to fulfil the prophecies. The doctrine of the virgin birth has been contradicted in the Gospel of Philip: *'Some say the Mary was impregnated by the grace of the Holy Spirit, / but they do not know what they say. / How could the Feminine impregnate the feminine?'* (Gospel of Philip, Plate 103) The idea of a God encompassing both the male and female was totally intolerable to the early Christian Church, founded as it was on the belief of a masculine deity!

- Yeshua was crucified between two bandits. They still showed signs of life when the Roman centurions came round to check on them, otherwise their limbs would not have been crushed, as was the custom. Jesus' limbs were not crushed, which meant that he was already dead, as far as the Roman centurions could ascertain. But the bandits had not been mercilessly scourged as Yeshua had, until the flesh was ripped and torn from his body. He was already totally exhausted before the crucifixion. Even the gospels record that he was very weak, as he sank down under the weight of the cross, and they had to get someone to help him carry it. It is easily believable, therefore, that Yeshua could have passed into a deep state of unconsciousness and apparent death. But remember! The silver cord has to detach before the final moment! Yeshua obviously passed into a state of unconsciousness so early that even Pilate doubted his death, and before he allowed him to be removed from the cross, he sent the Roman centurions to certify that he was indeed dead.

- Not any of the crucifixion tools were actually mortal. Yeshua's hands and feet were tightly bound with coarse, thick cords, so tightly that the circulation of blood would have stopped, and his limbs would have become numb. This is proven by the fact that when the nails were hammered into his hands, there was little or no bleeding. The blood was forced back to the brain and heart by the viciously tight bindings, and would have caused fits of apoplexy and deep swoonings.

- The wound with the spear in the side of Yeshua was not given as the final death blow. That spear wound was meant to signify if the corpse would show any signs of convulsions or life. The wound was close above the hip, made at an inclined angle, only piercing the skin, and not any internal organs. If Yeshua was already dead, the wound would not have spurted water and blood, as a dead corpse will not bleed from an external wound, the blood would be already congealed.

- The body of Yeshua was taken down very carefully from the cross by his Essene brothers, notably Nicodemus who was of the highest level within the Brotherhood, and their most advanced medical physician, and Joseph of Arimathea, referred to in the gospels as the rich man who buried Jesus in the tomb which he had prepared for himself. But other sources, such as Dolores Cannon's books on regression already referred to earlier, and Prentis and Wilsons' book 'The Essenes Children of the Light' tell a different story about Joseph of Arimathea, confirming what we saw earlier. They tell us he was the uncle of Yeshua, the brother of his mother Mary, and as well as being one of the most wealthy men in the known world, with his huge fleet of ships plying back and forth across the Mediterranean carrying tin from Cornwall for use in weaponry for the vast Roman armies, he was also a member of the Jewish Sanhedrin, the highest political authority in the land. So it was Joseph of Arimathea who gained permission from Pilate to take Yeshua down from the cross after a relatively short period of time. Even more significantly, though, and unknown to anyone else outside the Essene community, Joseph of Arimathea also belonged to the Brotherhood.

- The Essenes were advanced, expert healers. Yeshua was resuscitated by them in the tomb, as recorded in Dolores Cannon's book and again confirmed in Prentis and Wilson's books on regression. Yes, Jesus' spirit was far out of his body, but prepared coverings, saturated in aromatic herbs, aloe, spices and herbs were all administered to him by his Essene Brothers, restoring him to life in the tomb, and then removing him from that same tomb to a secret Essene place of refuge and safety.

- A dead corpse does not walk, does not talk, and it most definitely does not ask for food! But that is exactly what this supposed risen-from-the-dead body of Yeshua did! He asked for food, as recorded in the gospels, and his disciples gave him boiled fish to eat. Likewise, a spirit body does not bear wounds. But the supposed risen-from-the dead body of Jesus still bore the wounds of his persecution!

- Not all the Essene Brotherhood knew about these goings-on at the crucifixion. They all had their part to play. Only the core group surrounding Yeshua were in on the secrecy, and remember, if anyone could keep secrets, it was the Essenes! Secrecy was their second nature! We learn, again, from the previously mentioned books on regression, that the Essenes were positioned all along the earth energy ley-lines across Jerusalem, sending energy up to Yeshua on the cross, trying to keep the energy inside his torn and wearied body. And we also learn that those Essene Brothers around the crucifixion area, apart from the core group, were under strict instructions not to look as Yeshua was removed from the cross, and to forget what they had just seen and not ask any questions. This is made very specific and clear in 'Essenes Children of the Light' by Joanna Prentis and Stuart Wilson. This alone raises suspicions that something was going on which was kept secret from everyone except those most closely surrounding Yeshua.

- So the probability is that Yeshua did not actually die on the cross, but the message went out that he did and that he then resurrected. The Essenes had to spread this message, for Yeshua's own safety and survival, and of course, to fulfil the prophecies.

- But Yeshua could not have resurrected because he had not died in the first place! But how else were the Essenes going to make the prophecy of his resurrection come true?

- Theologians have long been telling us that the gospels are metaphoric and symbolic. So the death of Yeshua by crucifixion and his resurrection from the dead are symbolic of man's transcendence over death and continued life in the Spirit world, where infinity and immortality guarantee that the energy we are will never die. Energy cannot die, it cannot be killed, it can only be changed or transmuted. But why and how has it come about that millions of people across all continents still believe in the literal words of the gospels?

- And the Ascension! Did it ever happen? If we follow the theory that Jesus did not die on the cross, but was revived by his Essene friends, then the Ascension appears to be yet another made-up story, either by the gospel writers, or maybe by the Essenes themselves, who started the rumour that Jesus had ascended in order to throw his enemies off his trail for once and for all. Yes, the Essenes could keep secrets! And the truth about the death, resurrection and ascension of Yeshua has been the best kept secret ever!

- By the time the gospels and Acts were written, around 80 C.E., the Essenes as a sect were certainly facing a crisis. Their teachings and doctrines had been declared heresy and their sacred writings and texts were being destroyed, or at least those that had not been hidden. 'Gnosis', which means 'knowledge', became a heresy, and the early church doctrine of vicarious atonement, meaning the suffering and death undergone by Jesus to redeem mankind, became even more deeply entrenched in the minds of the masses. Jesus had replaced the sacrifice of animals with the sacrifice of himself, while the science of Pythagoras, Plato, and the truths of the ancient Mysteries, which he tried to teach us, were being obliterated.

So it is time for us, in this, the twenty-first century, 2,000 years after Yeshua ben Joseph walked amongst us as a teacher and healer to finally accept, that the Jesus presented to us by the early Christian Church never existed as such. Or it is time to at least question his existence! That Jesus in the gospels, that Jesus of the early Roman Christian Church is a composite figure, created by the early Roman Christian Church to solidify and unite the expansive and expanding Roman empire under the one banner of religion and religious beliefs. And in order to do so, that new religion had to compete with all the other Roman gods, most of whom were born of virgins, died and resurrected in order to save mankind. We must all, indeed, be well saved by now if that is the case! Yes, that early Roman Christian Church was just a re-hash of those very same superstitions and idolatry that Yeshua himself was teaching and preaching against! That was how it was 2,000 years ago! A different time, a different place, a different understanding from 2017!

It is time for us to be set free by the truth! The truth that Yeshua incarnated on Planet Earth 2,000 years ago to give us!

Yeshua incarnated into the secretive, mysterious Essene Brotherhood in order to fulfil his life mission this time around. Yeshua was, just like all of us, coming yet again to this dense energy earth plane with the veil pulled down firmly over his eyes. He had to learn like the rest of us, he did not come fully equipped with all the knowledge he needed. He had to work his way up there! He started just like us. There can be no violation of the natural universal laws!

And just like us, he chose those who would assist him in fulfilling his life mission. He chose to incarnate amongst the secretive, mysterious Essene Brotherhood.

And why?

Because, as we have seen throughout this book, they were the ones who carried the teachings and healings of the Ancient Mystery Schools, the very knowledge that Yeshua needed to get out to the people, the very knowledge that had and still is, being denied us by those in power who seek to control us for their own mercenary ends.

Yeshua was a human aspect of a great Spiritual being that exists beyond time and space. Not Jesus! Not Jesus of the early Roman Christian Church! But Yeshua! Yeshua ben Joseph! Essene teacher and healer!

The early Roman Christian Church turned him into a god, deifying him, manipulating him, their own political pawn, in their own political chess game, presenting to us Jesus the god-man, rather than a human being like us all! We are all of divine essence, we all carry the God spark within us, just like Yeshua. But this has been denied us in church teachings. According to the early Christian Church teaching, Jesus was god, and so far above us that we will never get to where he is at. But we are all going in that direction, up the spiritual escalator, some of us are just taking longer than others on the journey! Life is all about evolution. And there is no reverse gear in the evolutionary process! There can be no violation of the natural universal laws!

The Essene Brotherhood spawned, birthed, raised Yeshua, preparing him for his mission in fulfilling the ancient prophecies concerning the imminent arrival of a Messiah who would free the Jewish people from the hated Romans and return God's kingdom to earth. And those prophecies foretold that the Messiah would be crucified and die on the cross for all mankind.

We have seen, however, that this was not exactly what happened!

The Essene Community fostered Yeshua, fed, clothed and sheltered him throughout his mission of spreading their teachings, which carried the great truths, the great mysteries about the laws of creation, the laws of nature and its elements, the nature of humanity, the nature of life and the nature of God. They had communities and houses spread throughout many lands, and it was in these secret establishments that Jesus found refuge and nurturing during his mission. Yeshua had chosen, just like his cousin John the Baptist, to be an Essene traveler throughout the Galilee area spreading the good news, rather than remaining in any one Essene community, and as such, he had access to secret Essene households for nourishment, rest and refreshment.

Remember reading earlier in this book, in the chapter on the New Testament writings and Jesus, how Jesus was often at the home of Lazarus and his sisters Martha and Mary in Bethany? Remember reading how we have never been told by the gospels what went on there? How we have never been told the significance of that household?

Well, is it not now quite obvious that the house in Bethany to which Jesus often returned, was an Essene household, shrouded in mystery and secrecy as they all were? We know that Mary Magdalene herself was a member of the Essenes, again, like Yeshua, a member who chose to travel and spread the good news rather than live in any particular settled Essene community.

Yeshua was an Essene teacher and healer, sent out from the Essene Brotherhood to spread the teachings of '*The Way*', they themselves being '*Followers of The Way*'. And those teachings were so opposed to the beliefs of the Jewish people that Yeshua fell foul of the Pharisees, the Sadducees and the Priests of the Temple, all of whom saw in him a radical disturber seriously threatening their hold and power over the people, and in their eyes he had to be removed.

Yeshua, like all members of the Essene Brotherhood, believed in the truth of the ancient teachings, and was willing to accept death and martyrdom in pursuit of those truths and getting them out to the people. Yeshua willingly and freely chose this role as teacher, and knew that he would be crucified for it. Yeshua died for his belief in truth and for spreading that truth. He could well have listened to the pleas and requests of his disciples, concerned for his safety, to abandon his teaching mission and retreat to live a peaceful, trouble-free life in one or other of the Essene settlements. But that was not Jesus' way! He knew exactly what he was doing!

So Yeshua was crucified, fulfilling the prophecies. But! And this is a very big but! The laws of nature are unbreakable, inviolable, unconditional! No person can interfere with the sacred laws of nature. They are there for a reason! They hold all of creation together! Absolutely all of it! And we are all connected within those binding laws! What affects one, affects all. If the tiniest bit of those binding laws were to be interfered with, which cannot and will not be allowed to happen, then the whole of creation would collapse in chaos! That's why those natural universal and cosmic laws are there! To maintain creation throughout infinity, beyond time and space! And our free will is another of those irrefutable universal natural laws! God has not created the chaos in our present world! Nor can we question why God has allowed it to happen! We, and we alone, with our free will, have created our present world. And no God, no Jesus will interfere to save us from our own destruction! Only we ourselves can save ourselves from impending destruction! That's the universal law! Irrefutable! Unchangeable! Inviolable! Unconditional!

So no-one, no God, no Jesus, no person, no church, no matter what weapons it may claim to have stored in its theological arsenal, can violate any part of those natural laws! To say that

"*Nothing is impossible with God*", as many people do and will say, especially those in the upper echelons of the Church hierarchy, is just displaying an ignorance of the whole meaning behind creation, the nature of God and the nature of life. That is merely an opt-out clause for those who need such a safety-net, for those who cannot defend or explain their teachings, dogmas and doctrines!

And one of those natural, unbendable, inviolable natural laws says that once the silver cord, that spiritual cord that attaches the soul to the physical body is detached, then that soul, that spirit, cannot return to that same physical body.

As I asked before, can the butterfly return to be the caterpillar? Can the dragon-fly return to be the grub?

Yeshua appeared to return to his physical body. But the only way that was possible was that he was never actually dead in the first place!

Yes! Yeshua survived the crucifixion!

And how can I possibly make such a statement with such conviction?

By the line of argument I have just outlined above!

The Essene Brotherhood allowed the rumour to take hold, the rumour that spread rapidly amongst the superstitious Jewish people, that Yeshua had risen from the dead because they wanted to protect Yeshua. Likewise, the story of the ascension of the body of Yeshua into heaven! Remember! The natural laws of nature, of the universe and of the cosmos cannot and will not be violated by anyone!

Yeshua was spawned, birthed and raised by the Essenes to fulfil his role as the crucified Messiah! Like a child born to be king, he was taught and prepared for his inevitable destiny. His inevitable destiny as the crucified Messiah!

Lamb to the slaughter! And as such, Yeshua deserves our deepest compassion!

And Yeshua died for his daring to spread the truth amongst the Jewish people! And for that he deserves our deepest admiration and gratitude!

Yeshua was not the supernatural son of a supernatural god, endowed with supernatural powers. He was human, just like all who incarnate on this earth plane, and just like all who incarnate on this earth plane, he was subject to the universal natural laws.

And as a human, he had to face the terrible fear that engulfed him in the Garden of Gethsemane. The terrible fear that tomorrow he was to be crucified! No wonder the sweat broke out on him! He was a human being, facing crucifixion, to be nailed to a cross in a few hours time. The fear that he was on his own, that God had somehow deserted him:

"Oh my Father, if it is your will, let this cup pass from me!"

But this was immediately followed by:

"Not my will, but thine be done!"

And on the cross:

"Father, forgive then for they know not what they do!"

And:

"Father, into thy hands I commend my spirit."

Yeshua, just like us, had his human side and his Spiritual side. But he was able to differentiate between the two. He knew that his human side, his ego, was trying to dominate, to be the stronger, and he was able to transcend that and reach his Christ Consciousness zone.

We do not know at what point in his life Jesus achieved self-mastery. But as we have seen throughout this book, he most probably was exposed to the teachings of the great Spiritual and intellectual masters of the world. However, that alone could not have achieved self-mastery for him. Teachings, dogmas and doctrines are only the tools in helping to achieve self-mastery. They, in themselves, are not the ultimate goal. Self-mastery for Jesus, as for any of us, has to come from within. Jesus achieved self-mastery from an inner awakening, an inner realisation that he was of divine essence, that he was of the divinity of God. At some point, Jesus made the connection between himself and God, attaining the Christ Consciousness, the God within himself, and therefore operating on a much higher consciousness level. It was the Christ Consciousness within him, and his attaining of that Christ Consciousness within himself that differentiated Jesus from those around him. But again, as we have seen, Jesus did not arrive on this earth plane already attuned to the Christ Consciousness within himself. Jesus was subject to the natural laws of this planet and of the cosmos just as we all are. What Jesus tried to teach us is that we all have the Christ Consciousness Spiritual energy within ourselves. It was Jesus who taught us that life is all about a change in consciousness, a transformation to a higher Spiritual state of consciousness, which enables us to recognise and accept the divinity in us all and not just in Jesus.

And that was what he came to teach us! How to attain our own individualised Christ Consciousness!

Yeshua does not need to reincarnate again on this earth plane. And why not?

Simply because he is working through each one of us, helping us to attain our Individualised Christ Consciousness energy level while here on earth. And as more and more of us attain that level of consciousness, that is how heaven will come on earth.

Substantially changing the collective consciousness of mankind is an on-going process that extends over millennia, and requiring the participation of many generations. It was this process that Yeshua started 2,000 years ago, when he sowed the seeds, the seeds that are now sprouting. Yeshua was a child of his time, brought up in the traditions of his nation, the Jewish nation, into which he freely chose to incarnate. The traditions of the Jewish people and the ancient prophecies had profound influence on his life and instinctively guided many of his actions. But it was the secretive and mysterious Essene Brotherhood who nurtured him as one of their own teachers, teaching the ancient truths to the people, and it was in teaching those truths, those truths which we are once again finding today, for which Yeshua sacrificed his own life.

That's how important the truth is!

Important enough for Yeshua to die for!

Important enough for a highly evolved soul to return to the earth plane! And to suffer persecution in teaching us that truth!

That truth that will set us all free! Free from the confining, restricting bonds of controlling religions!

And by giving us back those ancient truths, Yeshua saved humanity from spending countless more centuries stuck in the death consciousness level, the base consciousness awareness level, the lowest energy dimension, where humanity was when he came to earth 2,000 years ago. Yeshua loved humanity with such unconditional love that he was, literally, prepared to die in getting the truth to us!

What a debt we owe to Yeshua!

And how can we ever repay that debt?

We can repay that debt by accepting the truths he came here to teach us! And by accepting those truths, we will allow each and every individual soul to fly freely and sing its own glorious, rapturous song, its own individualised and unique chord, its own melodious note, in the harmonised, synchronised orchestra of the cosmos and throughout the vastness of the entirety of creation.

That is all Yeshua asks of us!

Until we meet again!

Namaste!

Eileen McCourt

EPILOGUE

I am Ascended Master Sananda.

I am now a Completed One. An Ascended One. One in total Enlightenment. One in total wholeness, complete awareness. One of the Order of Melchizedek, a highly evolved and advanced service order of teachers. I am one of the members of the High Council and of the Universal Lords.

I reside here with all the other members of the Great White Brotherhood. We operate throughout many levels and many planetary systems.

Here, for me now, is an energy vibrational frequency, a sublime, ecstatic state of wholeness, a state of completedness. Complete consciousness, complete soul awareness.

Here, we know only love. Love and Light.

Here, we are whole. Whole and complete.

Here, we are devoted to helping other souls achieve what we have achieved, - total merging with Source, total merging into the Light. We work to help all mankind, to raise the spiritual consciousness of all humanity.

My *last incarnation on the Planet Earth frequency was as Yeshua ben Joseph, known to you as Jesus the Nazarene. To open up the path for you I had to tread the path myself. When I left this highest of vibrations 2,000 years ago to descend to the density of form, the density of matter, in a human body, on Planet Earth, I ushered in a new cycle, the cycle of Pisces. Now that cycle too has ended, and the cycle of Aquarius has begun. But not everyone has made the leap. It is an enormous transition from Pisces to*

Aquarius, and cannot be imposed on any person by external forces. It must come from within. That is the seed I sowed 2,000 years ago, and it is now starting to bloom and flourish. 2,000 years is a long time in human terms, but it is only a thought here where I am.

We here in the highest vibrational energy levels within the Great Universal God Consciousness could change the world in the blink of a human eye. We could restore Planet Earth to the status of Atlantis. We could establish Utopia, Elysium, heaven on earth. And we would so love to do that! But that is not the way Divine law works. Man has free will! That most unalterable, that most sacred, that most precious of all gifts!

We can only guide from here, into the hearts of those who are ready. I was not born enlightened 2,000 years ago, contrary to what the gospels have taught! I had to find my way to Spiritual enlightenment, to raised Spiritual consciousness, just as everyone else born into the earth plane. I too was subject to the laws of the earth!

People 2,000 years ago were not yet spiritually ready for what I was teaching. Now, 2,000 years later, there is a greater awareness amongst humanity. Humanity as a whole has grown in consciousness, and many amongst you now are ready for the inner teachings, unlike when I was last on earth, when I had to teach mostly through parables.

We here in the higher Spiritual vibrational levels use different methods of teaching now. That's because the physical Planet Earth has changed so much. When I incarnated as Yeshua, teachings were passed down orally, to save them from falling into the wrong hands. But they have fallen into the wrong hands anyway! Simply because many of those who were given the knowledge, instead of sharing and teaching the masses, sought power for themselves and retained that knowledge, corrupting the whole system.

But now, the knowledge is spreading to where it is meant to spread. Modern technology and media methods are all used by us to get our message across. We use every means and every person whose consciousness is open to us. But none of us here can violate the divine law of free will!

I am no different from everyone else! I am an individualised version of the great Universal Consciousness of God, just like each and every other life-force. I am just further along the path to Oneness, to Completion, to full Awareness. That's why I can help you. I have already been where you now are!

But I can only guide you! I can only hold the ladder of Ascension for you.

Mankind so needs to move beyond fear into love. That 'little me', that human ego that constantly pushes itself to the fore, needs to be put aside so that each and every soul can be reborn as the 'Greater I' the 'I AM' of the Spirit, the 'I AM' of the Universal Christ Consciousness, which unites all in the Oneness of all creation. If only each person could see that by shelving the ego, they are not losing their freedom. By shelving and abandoning the ego, they are actually freeing themselves from the restrictions of a small confining space, limited potentiality, a tiny microcosm, to emerge into the vastness of the macrocosm of the 'I AM' where potentiality is unlimited. That's the real meaning of freedom! That's the real meaning of truth!

Humanity was not yet ready 2,000 years ago to make this great leap of courage. People then wanted and needed a reassuring, a comforting form of religion, rather than a challenging form of spirituality. They needed someone, some external institution to make the laws for them, set the rules, and promise salvation if those rules were adhered to. And where a great need arises, there are always those who are waiting, only too ready and willing to step in and take control. And so it was 2,000 years ago that they founded a church, a religion in my name. Founding that church and that religion in my name was merely a matter of convenience and opportunism.

They deified and mythologised me. They distorted my teachings about the great truths, which I had come to earth to teach. The great truths which would set mankind free. They made me into a god to compete with their other false beliefs. BUT! They kept my name out there! Many other great masters have disappeared under the shifting sands of time!

But they created a false God, an authoritarian, a judgemental, punishing god, who demanded constant appeasement and atonement. They made people believe that illness was sent to them by God for their sins! They set themselves up as the sole authority, the sole link, the sole mediator between man and God.

Great minds in the Renaissance knew something was not right! How well they knew! We were able to impress upon them, to enlighten them how to get the message out. They embedded many clues in their works, clues which many humans are now finding. Those brave men could not openly defy those who distorted my teachings, so they had to find another way in order to safeguard their lives. Look at the painting of the Last Supper for example! My beloved Mary Magdalene, my twin soul! She is right there, on my right hand!

How they have castigated my beloved Mary over the last 2,000 years! But she is now having her say! Her story is being told. The world will soon know and understand the debt they owe to her. She anchored the Light on Planet Earth with me. Opened up the density of Planet Earth to receive the Light. Yes! She was there alongside me all the time. Times when I despaired of ever getting through to people, times when I felt so frustrated with their closed minds. Times when I felt angry with them. Times when I just wanted to abandon my mission.

Today, people have a stronger spiritual sense and are no longer being taken in by those distorted teachings of the so-called Christian churches.

I did not do all those things they said I did! I did not die on that cross to save mankind from sin! To redeem mankind! That is what these so-called Christian churches are teaching! How wrong it all is! Only each one of you can do that for yourself!

Let me be very specific here! I came to found neither a new religion nor a new church! I came to teach people the great truths which had been lost to them down through the ages. I came as a Spiritual teacher. I came to set people free. Free from the superstitions and false gods that held them in chains and bondage.

And what great truths did I come to teach?

The great truths about the nature of God, of humanity, about the Oneness of all creation, of life and death, of the kingdom of God being within each and every one of us. The great truths about the energy that we all are, the subtle energy fields that permeate the entire cosmos, each affecting all others. The great truths that we create our own reality by the thoughts and words we send out into those energy fields surrounding us, attracting the same energy type back to us. The great truths that God does not need to forgive us, because karma takes care of all that! Each and every person will balance his own actions through the unavoidable wheel of karma, no-one excepted. That is the great universal law! And like all universal laws, unavoidable, inviolable, unstoppable! What you give out, you get back! And there are most definitely no exceptions, no exceptions whatsoever, to that rule!

So my crucifixion on the cross had nothing whatsoever to do with me saving mankind! Where did they get all this? I certainly did not teach it!

I was crucified because I was teaching these great truths to the ordinary people. And because I was teaching those truths, I ran foul of those Jewish authorities whose very existence depended on the people not knowing those truths. I knew I would be killed for what I was doing! I had no doubt about that!

But my mission 2,000 years ago in first-century Jewish Palestine was to teach those truths! There could be no compromise! People had drifted so far off the spiritual path. In fact, so far off the spiritual path that they were just not yet ready. But I sowed the seeds! Seeds that take a long time to sprout and grow! That time has now arrived! And each and every life-force now in a physical embodiment on Planet Earth at this most momentous time in the history of humanity, has freely and willingly chosen to be there to play a vital part in this current raising of the earth's vibration.

And for that, we here in the highest echelons of the Spiritual vibrational energy frequencies applaud you all and thank you! We need you all right now more than ever to fulfil this great joint *task of raising the Spiritual consciousness of all humanity onto a higher vibrational level, a huge move towards Planet Earth's ascension.*

They say I will come again in the clouds for a final judgement of all souls. Where has that come from? They just did not understand! I was talking about the Spiritual kingdom. I told them my kingdom is not of the earth plane, but they did not understand. Yes, I will come again, but it will be in men's hearts.

Continue to do as you are currently doing! Continue to hold yourself in your Individualised Christ Consciousness zone, and do not allow any of the lower energy frequencies which are very prevalent on earth right now to pull you down to their level. Rise above all negativity! And do not beat yourself up over the current state of the world and feel that you should be doing something about it! The only way the world will change for the better is when enough individual people have managed to raise themselves up into their Individualised Christ Consciousness zone. And neither you, me, nor anyone else can pull them up or force them! Only they themselves can do that! And when a sufficient number of people have attained their Christ Consciousness level, then, and then only, will heaven come to earth!

Peace be with you!

Eileen McCourt

JESUS LOST AND FOUND

BIBLIOGRAPHY

Aslan, Reza, 'Zealot' (Westbourne Press)

Baigent, Michael, 'The Jesus Papers', (Harper Collins)

Baigent , Michael, and Richard Leigh, 'The Dead Sea Scrolls Deception', (Arrow Publications)

Butz, Jeffrey, 'The Brother of Jesus and the Lost Teachings of Christianity', (Inner Traditions)

Cannon, Dolores, 'Jesus and the Essenes', (Ozark Mountain)

Cannon, Dolores, 'They Walked with Jesus', (Ozark Mountain)

Cayce, Edgar, 'Story of Jesus' Selected and edited by Jeffrey Furst (Berkley Books)

Churton, Tobias, ' The Mysteries of John the Baptist' (Inner Tradition)

Churton, Tobias, 'The Missing Family of Jesus' (Watkins)

Crossan, John Dominic, 'Jesus: A Revolutionary Biography' (Harper One)

Ehrman, Bart D. 'Did Jesus Exist?' (Harper One)

Ehrman, Bart D. 'Jesus - Apocalyptic Prophet Of The New Millennium' (Oxford University Press)

Ehrman, Bart D. 'How Jesus Became God' (Harper One)

Eisenham, Robert, ' James the Brother of Jesus', (Watkins)

Ewing, Upton Clang, 'The Prophet of the Dead Sea Scolls: The Essenes and the Early Christians- One and the Same People'

Fortune, Dion, 'Glastonbury, Avalon of the Heart' (Weiser)

Heartsong, Claire, 'Anna, Grandmother of Jesus', (S.E.E.Publishing)

Heartsong, Claire, 'Anna, The Voice of the Magdalenes' (S.E.E. Publishing)

Johnson, Luke Timothy, 'The Real Jesus', (Harper One)

Jowett, George, 'The Drama of the Lost Disciples', (Covenant)

Leloup, Jean-Yves, 'The Gospel of Philip', (Inner Traditions)

Leloup, Jean-Yves, 'The Gospel of Thomas', (Inner Traditions)

Leloup, Jean-Yves, 'The Gospel of Mary Magdalene', (Inner Traditions)

Leloup, Jean-Yves, 'Judas and Jesus', (Inner Traditions)

Maccoby, Hyam, 'The Myth-Maker: Paul and the Invention of Christianity', (Harper and Row)

McCannon, Tricia, 'Jesus: The Explosive Story of the Lost 30 Years And The Ancient Mystery Religions' (Hampton Roads)

Michaels, Kim, 'Walking the Mystical Path of Jesus' (More to Life)

Michaels, Kim, 'The Mystical Teachings of Jesus' (More to Life)

Michaels, Kim, 'Climbing Higher on the Mystical Path' (More to Life)

Olson, Carl E., 'Did Jesus Really Rise from the Dead?' (Ignatius Press)

Padgett, James E, 'True Gospel Revealed Anew By Jesus' Vols. 1,2,3,4 (Church of the New Birth)

Price, Dennis, 'The Missing Years of Jesus' (Hay House)

Prophet, Elizabeth Clare, 'The Lost Years of Jesus' (Summit University Press)

Sanders, E.P. 'The Historical Figure of Jesus' (Penguin)

Smyth, Alexander, ' The Occult Life of Jesus of Nazareth'

Stanford, Peter, 'Judas: The troubling history of the renegade apostle (Hodder)

Szekely, Edmond Bordeaux, 'The Gospel of the Essenes' (The C.W. Daniel Company)

Tabor, James D. 'The Jesus Dynasty' (Harper Element)

Sutton, Neal, 'Buried by the Church' (Matador Books)

Unterbrink, Daniel T. 'Judas of Nazareth: How the Greatest Teacher of First-Century Israel was Replaced by a Literary Creation', (Bear and Company)

Vermes, Geza, 'The Complete Dead Sea Scrolls in English', (Penguin)

Vermes, Geza, 'Christian Beginnings'

Vermes, Geza, 'The Changing Faces of Jesus', (Penguin)

Vermes, Geza, 'The Authentic Gospel Of Jesus' (Penguin)

Vermes, Geza, 'The Religion of Jesus The Jew' (Fortress Press)

Vining, Marvin, 'Jesus the Wicked Priest: How Christianity was born of an Essene Schism', (Bear and Company)

Wilson, Stuart, and Joanna Prentis, 'Essenes- Children of the Light', (Ozark Mountain)

Wiilson, Stuart, and Joanna Prentis, 'The Magdalene Version' (Ozark Mountain)

Wilson, Stuart, and Joanna Prentis, 'Power of the Magdalene' (Ozark Mountain)

Wright, Tom, 'Simply Jesus' (Society for Promoting Christian Knowledge)

Made in the USA
Columbia, SC
27 June 2017